REBEL AND SAGE

Tom Heron: 'Rebel and Sage'

Rebel and Sage

A Biography of Tom Heron, 1890–1983

JOHN S. PEART-BINNS
&
GILES HERON

Pentland Books
Edinburgh – Cambridge – Durham – USA

First published in 2001 by
Pentland Books Ltd
1 Hutton Close
South Church
Bishop Auckland
Durham

Email: manuscripts@pentlandpress.co.uk
Web: www.pentlandpress.co.uk

ISBN 1–85821-867–5

Typeset in Adobe Garamond 11 on 13
by Carnegie Publishing
Carnegie House
Chatsworth Road
Lancaster
LA1 4SL

www.carnegiepub.co.uk

Printed and bound by
Antony Rowe Ltd
Chippenham

Contents

Appendices

Illustrations

Author's Note

THE DUAL AUTHORSHIP OF THIS BOOK has been of the tandem variety, not a duet. John Peart-Binns was already an established biographer while writing a draft version between 1981 and 1986. Giles Heron only took up the cudgels seriously in 1997, adding substantial sections, re-writing and editing the rest with a free hand thanks to the generosity of his colleague. John Peart-Binns was able to draw on years of professional research into the background of the twentieth-century movements and figures that constitute the Church Militant in its widest and least ecclesiastical sense.

Giles Heron's advantages have been complementary. One is that much of the story of this book is also the story of his own life. Another that the passage of ten years has already sharpened historical perspective, as the cycle of fashion brings various issues back into relevance. A further advantage has been the continual emergence of fresh first-hand evidence, thanks to two family traditions, the enjoyment of letter writing and hoarding the fruits like squirrels.

The gestation period of this biography has extended to close on twenty years, during which time each author in turn enjoyed invaluable and unstinted assistance from a great many people, some of whom are no longer living.

The absence of the customary list, thanking them individually, is not evidence that their help was taken for granted; rather that an attempt to record it in detail would be inadequate and incomplete. Their proper reward was, and is, the knowledge that they were helping to create a tribute and a little piece of history that could so easily have remained an unfulfilled dream.

We are deeply indebted to them all.

Acknowledgements

The following have kindly agreed to allow extracts from the writings of associates of Tom Heron to be reproduced here:

Mrs Valerie Elliot, Mrs Roslyn Thistlewood, Dr Roger Slack, Mr David Leach, Mr Philip Conford, Mr Benedict Read, Professor George Wedell, Dr Tom Osborn, Mr Michael Gambling. Quotations from writings, whether published or unpublished, of the late Miss Dorothy L. Sayers have been reproduced here by kind permission of Messrs David Higham Associates.

We have also received gracious permission to include extracts from Mr Alan Powers' book, *Modern Block Printing of Textiles*, Walker Books, London, 1992, from Mrs Joy Wragg's book, *One Life Amid Many*, Regency Press, London, and to include further quotations from *The Welwyn and Hatfield Times*, *The Pottery Gazette and Glass Trade Review* and *The Agricultural History Review*.

Further quotations have been included from the following, now sadly deceased: Mr Jack Eastwood, Mr Maurice Reckitt, Mr Patrick McLaughlin, Dr J. Vowles, Miss Dorothy Emmet, Sir John Lawrence, Mr J.H. Oldham, Mr Philip Marriott and the Revd. Canon V. A. Demant.

Illustration Acknowledgements

The portrait of Tom Heron by Bruce Turner on p. 16 is reproduced by kind permission of Leeds Museum and Art Galleries.

The design 'Cherry Orchard' by Paul Nash on p. 50 is reproduced by kind permission of the artist and of The Decorative Arts Society and the Victoria and Albert Museum.

The photos of the two Cresta shops on pp. 53 and 55 are reproduced by kind permission of the executors of the late Mr McKnight Kauffer and also of the *Journal of the Decorative Arts Society 1890–1940* and also by the courtesy of The British Architectural Library of the Royal Institute of British Architects.

The photo of a Welwyn Garden City street scene on p. 81 is included by kind permission of the photographer, Mr Ken Wright, and also of Welwyn Garden City Society.

Miss Katharine and Miss Susanna Heron have graciously permitted us to reproduce the works by Mr Patrick Heron.

For the sketch entitled 'Tom Heron asleep in armchair, 1983' we are indebted to the artist, Mrs Margaret Heron.

Introduction

'Late one cold April afternoon I was motoring home over Bodmin Moor when ahead of me on a very isolated stretch of the road I saw a man huddled up on a pile of stones gazing into the driving rain. He did not move at all as I passed him but remained looking straight in front of him. As there were no cattle in sight I naturally came to the conclusion that something must be wrong, and pulling up, walked back to see if I could be of any assistance. He paid no attention to me as I approached and did no more than shake his head when I asked him if anything were the matter. He was of the tramp class, obviously about seventy years of age, and judging that he was suffering from exposure I enquired which way he was going. "I ain't going," he said. Puzzled by this answer I then asked what the devil he was doing. For a moment he looked at me as if undecided whether to reply or no, and then a smile came over his face and with slow deliberation he said: "I know it sounds silly, but I put my first strength into that." I looked in the direction where his hand pointed, and I saw nothing. "Into what?" I shouted. "Into that railway embankment," he said. "It was my first job as a young man."

'By this time I was feeling almost as wet through as he was, but I did not like the idea of leaving him alone. How long did he intend to sit there? He didn't know. How long had he been there? Since morning. Where was he going to spend the night? He didn't know. I persuaded him that there was another day tomorrow and that I could drop him near Camborne workhouse, so he consented to come along with me. On the way we stopped at a pub, where I found that he was really hungry. And as he ate one thick sandwich after another, he told me the story of his life. His father and mother had deserted him when he was a boy of eleven. For four or five years he had earned his living by begging in the streets, selling matches, or doing other "boy's" jobs. From the north of England he had drifted down to Cornwall and one spring day, hearing that navvies were wanted on the new railway, he had plucked up courage and offered himself. The foreman had been sceptical, but he had kept his place. He told me how wonderful it was that men could build such great things as railway embankments. He said that often as he had watched holiday trains leave the big cities, he had wondered if they were going to use his embankment. Did I think that by now a million people had been taken over it? Ten years ago he had made Newquay the goal of his summer tramp because he had been told that most of the holiday makers who went to Cornwall went there, and he wanted to see them enjoying themselves. And during the last winter, which he had spent in a Lancashire workhouse, he had had an irresistible desire to go down to Cornwall again and, before he died, see for the last time the job into which he had "put his first strength."

'I had often come across the painter's pride of possession in his work and had grasped its significance, but many a time I had been worried by the egotism which went with it and marred it. This old man's satisfaction had no connection with pride. It was elemental, born of that humility which consists of seeing things as they really are. I had noticed that the painter retained his sense of ownership even though his picture had legally passed into the possession of another. The old tramp had never even bothered his head about the ownership of what he had made. I had realized that the artist's motive was really the impulse to work because something within him compelled him to get it out – he would perish if he didn't, and I had always thought that labourers and navvies worked from a lesser motive – pressure of circumstance from without. Yet this old man had "put his first strength" into a railway embankment, and by his reward I knew that his act had become a part of reality: "Mine elect shall long enjoy the work of their hands." '

THE ABOVE RECORD OF AN ENCOUNTER on Bodmin Moor was not intentionally autobiographical. It was part of the introduction to a book on the nature of work that Tom Heron was commissioned to write but never finished or published. Nevertheless it serves admirably to introduce him to our readers, giving them a first sip from which to gauge the flavour of the man and of the people and situations he dealt with. This book will focus on those people and situations as well as on the story of his life, for in addition to its biographical rôle it is conceived as a source of illumination of a period.

Heron lived an exciting life in exciting times. He played a part in many of the post-Victorian movements that shaped the twentieth century. Though in most cases those parts were small, they gain in significance by being linked together in the life of one person. He became involved in the challenge to established social and religious order thrown down by such revolutionary developments as socialism, women's suffrage, religious free-thinking and modern art, to name but some of the most prominent.

Although a man of vision, Heron was ever athirst for reality; a man of ideas and ideals, but also a man of action. His indomitable optimism led him to regard the disappearance of traditional certainties not as threatening loss but as opening up opportunities, so he plunged into each wave of change with remarkable relish and confidence.

Many people regret that idealism is largely squeezed out of their bread-earning, workaday lives and finds scope only in the concerns of their free time. There was no such dichotomy for Heron. The succession of his full-time business responsibilities expressed the full range of his ideals, social, economic and artistic, especially in creating Cresta Silks Limited and in conceiving the famous Utility Clothing scheme and administering it at the Board of Trade. Conversely his contribution to a great many idealistic movements included down-to-earth practical organization and hard work. For him work and play were first cousins as were the tragedy and comedy of the human condition.

A precociously early involvement in social issues at one end of life and an evergreen interest and open-mindedness surviving to the other, account for his active participation in public affairs for approaching eighty years. He who felt awe on seeing Ruskin in Coniston village, who remembered his parents lamenting the death of Gladstone, and who, visiting Islington Workhouse in 1906, watched with horror as 200 uniformed children filed in to their meal in unnatural silence, lived to regret a Thatcher Government's acceptance of unemployment and to respond with a poem to man's landing on the moon. The conscientious objector of the First World War protested to *The Times* about the arms trade protracting the war in Vietnam.

Tom Heron disliked labels, and no single label will stick to him. Throw one at him – poet, businessman, pacifist, monetary reformer, environmentalist, Christian sociologist, provocateur – and it covers more than it reveals. There is something enigmatic and elusive about him despite a forthrightness of manner and his self-revealing poetry and prose. The natural ardour of his character and the bent of his early inclinations led him to experience the funnel of failure as well as the spiral of success. Quixotic honesty is the reason for his steady refusal to 'run in harness.' As a speaker on public platform, street corner or in discussion circle, he was like a pepper cruet, giving relish to the palates of his audience. But as a poet his is the salt that preserves and purifies.

There may be no labels that will stick, but there is something that pervaded and enveloped him, namely, his Christian faith and undiluted commitment to the Church of England, which nurtured and strengthened him even when it exasperated him. Because of this, 'serving' is one thread which gives unity to Tom Heron. But it is not serving in the generally accepted sense of this over-used and much abused word. Throughout his life and manifold activities he sought and discovered the 'rhythm of the work' and then 'served the work.' What this means will become evident as the life of over ninety years unfolds. Suffice it here to comment that serving the work is not a catchpenny phrase. It is sacramental. It is also revolutionary.

Half Scot by blood, and proud of it, Heron was also very English. It should become evident to the reader that as a fearless reformer, he owed much to the tradition going back through Chesterton and Dickens to Cobbett, with all of whom he shared an exuberance of language. Those who had the good fortune to know him well sometimes fancied they could trace the ancestry of his humour in fact and fiction to Pepys and Falstaff, to Bunyan's *Pilgrim's Progress* and to those other pilgrims painted by Chaucer on their road to Canterbury.

Now it is time to trace the steps of Heron's own pilgrimage.

Chapter One

Harnessing Exuberance

Tom Heron was a complex and lively mixture of romantic and businessman, poet and sage, medievalist and innovator. The supporter and campaigner for the suffragette was also a chauvinist. The clubbable man on his feet was also a man of prayer on his knees. Unknown ancestors influenced him. In a genealogical quest he sought the larger-than-life figures, found a few, and came to the conclusion expressed in the opening line of one of his poems:

'The Heron race were lawless and hot-tempered.'

Then there was a great-uncle by marriage whose monument in the grounds of St Wilfrid's Church, Calverley, Bradford, bears the inscription: *In affectionate remembrance of Matthew Balme, who died August 26th 1884, aged 71 years: Defend the Poor and Fatherless: Do Justice to the Afflicted and Needy.*

This memorial was erected by factory operatives and personal friends in grateful recognition of Balme's zealous advocacy of the Ten Hours Bill. Matthew Balme (1813–1884) was a factory reformer concerned with 'the physical, social and moral improvement of factory workers.' Did Tom Heron see himself as a latter-day Matthew Balme? That he admired him there is no doubt.

Thomas Milner Heron, the fourth and penultimate child of Edmund and Annie Heron, was born on 3rd January 1890. His ancestors came from the Border country of England and Scotland. The colourful lawlessness of earlier times had given way to another strain, more Scottish than English, aptly and potently described in a family Bible presented to Tom's grandfather, Thomas Heron (1813–1895): 'Buy the truth and sell it not.' Leaving aside the philosophical question whether truth is bought, given or received, it is an interesting phrase.

The majority of Tom Heron's immediate forebears were men who had made their own way into positions of respect and prominence, yet none became public servants on a national, county or even local level. Were they a little too independent for that? The thought will recur in considering Tom Heron's own life. It was his grandfather who, with many Scotsmen, left the struggling borderlands to seek his fortune in the promising pastures of Bradford in the early nineteenth century, and he had the good sense to marry a Yorkshire girl. Subsequently the wool of the sheep was the only pastoral aspect of the Industrial Revolution which made Bradford the woollen centre of the world.

Edmund Heron (1851–1937) was born in Bradford, where he lived until 1913. He then went to live at Eastby, near Skipton, on the edge of the Yorkshire Dales. When he died, an obituary in a local paper described him accurately:

'Mr Heron was neither saint nor hero. He was made of good common human stuff that weathered well. His feet were firmly planted on the earth. The qualities that helped him through a long life, uneventful but not without its troubles, were not high-faluting ones, but sound and fundamental – honesty, industry, reliability, tolerance and charitableness in his judgement of men and his view of affairs, unfailing good humour and the tone of a good joke.

'He was no rebel or ardent reformer; he believed in a steady progress within the established order of things. His life was governed by a sense of duty to his God and to his neighbours. He never talked religion but it lay at the root of his life. He never wavered in it, nor lost his grip of it. It was this that gave him an equableness and cheerfulness through all the ups and downs of life and helped him to bear so gallantly, among other troubles, the smashing up of his business by the war, the tragic death of his eldest son (Edmund Franklin Heron) and the years of suffering of a much-loved invalid wife.'

Even allowing for obiturial excess, there are few signs here of a hot-tempered race who were regularly in trouble with the authorities. Yet his son, Tom, developed into a persistent rebel and ardent reformer. Here the initial influence came from his mother, though more by example than by precept. She had an enquiring, adventurous mind with an interest in contemporary affairs, even if she was tied to homemaking. Annie Milner had married Edmund Heron in 1884. She was the daughter of Joshua Milner, a long-established woollen draper and tailor in Bradford. Tom Heron always thought of her as a freethinker with a weakness for Roman Catholic ritual, in complementary contrast to her husband, who was an elder of the Presbyterian Church in Salem Street, Bradford, where the family worshipped. The church was not in the most salubrious of areas and attracted many people from the nearby slums. Appearances were deceptive for some of these people went not for religious reasons but because the church was warm and dry on cold, dark, dank nights. Sermons were long and further lengthened after lunch in the Heron household when that morning's sermon would be dissected and discussed. The suggestion is of a serious but not pious family.

As he grew up, Tom Heron took a Sunday-school class of young children when the superintendent found himself short of a teacher. It was quickly apparent that he had a rich imagination and a lively respect for the gospel stories. This was particularly noticeable after he was 'converted' at a mission service in Bradford led by the then famous evangelist, Gypsy Smith. Although his comprehension of God varied over a long life, there was never a time when he did not believe in God. Allegiance to the Church was a different matter, as we shall discover.

One of the major themes interwoven in the fabric of this book is the doctrine of work. In his unfinished book on the subject, Heron draws from the well of his own upbringing, offers insights into his early life and explains the course of his working life. The words may be reflective, but the examples are fresh. He wrote:

'I can well remember the first time I puzzled my head about the meaning of work.

The impression of Bradford on Patrick Heron aged 12.

It was when I was about six years old. I lived in a world which had mill " 'ands" at the bottom of the garden. If you were a visitor, the clatter of their clogs woke you up at half-past five in the morning as they hurried to the big mill. We did not talk much about them, but once I noticed that my mother seemed on the defensive when I asked a question about them. That set me off ... From my parents I learnt that the poor had to work hard if they were to avoid starvation, that they got used to discomfort and hardship because God was both wise and all-powerful and Jesus loved the poor, that somehow or other they must have deserved their lot – either they or their forebears must have sinned, that, nevertheless, I was to be kind to them, and that, in any case, I should understand all about it when I grew older. My father 'went to business', and so did the fathers of the other children I played with. But we could not help coming into contact with the 'working-class' children. My first contacts with them were conditioned by fear. The big strike which had taken place a few years before had resulted in rioting and assaults on the police, and the special constable's baton which was kept in a cupboard upstairs had served to impress upon me that the working classes could do a lot of harm to the businessmen if only they turned their roughness on to their masters instead of drinking and fighting amongst themselves. And so for a time I carefully avoided getting into a situation where I should have to fight a slum kid. But one day I had to fight a slum kid and I won. That made a lot of difference to my world. I felt more confident about life and though my mother took much of the pleasure out of my triumph by explaining that I ought to be stronger than my adversary because I had had better food and nourishment, I still rejoiced in the discovery of my superiority. From that time I began to have friends amongst the working-class boys and it was from Charlie, the washerwoman's son, that I got my next piece of philosophy about work. He was a year older than I was, but I was both bigger and stronger than he. One day he said proudly, 'I start half-time on Monday'. 'Where?', said I. 'At Drummond's', said he, 'It's an awful hard shop. The foreman's a devil.' Here was Charlie actually longing to begin work in a dreadful mill. More than once as I had walked past the mill and heard the heavy sound of machinery, I had uttered a prayer that God might save both my parents and me from committing whatever sins brought working in the mill as their just punishment. So I asked more questions about work and learnt that it was something hard and unpleasant, but nevertheless, something which every grown man must necessarily encounter.'

Occasionally Heron wondered if Drummond's would be his fate. When the subject of Charlie was debated in the family 'parliament' which mealtimes so often became, Heron learned that a man's work, though it ought to be hard and very often was bound to be unpleasant, was nevertheless something to which he should now be looking forward. It was impressed upon him that money was going to be spent on his education so that when the time came for him to tackle his real work in the world, he should have no excuse if he failed to render a good account of himself. Both his mother's and father's family histories were drawn upon for examples of successes and failures. He may have been muddled about the long-term advantages which had come to his grandfather from 'buying wool at the right time', and the equally lasting disadvantages which had befallen an uncle who had been, 'too soft-hearted for the grocery trade', yet he started to brace himself for the future.

First, Heron had to be educated. He entered Bradford Grammar School in 1901. With his eager bearing and bright eyes, one sees a boy with a zeal and zest for life. He showed an early interest in reading good literature. His grasp of themes and technical arguments was good. English was the queen of subjects to feed the mind and kindle the imagination and, most of all, to be used – the correct spelling of words was of less importance. There was something romantic about the sweep of history – never mind about the learning, recitation and regurgitation of dates. He liked French and showed promise in German.

This lively boy had good, if erratic, results. The Science results fell below the Arts in examinations. He loved an argument and did not restrict this to the school debating society, where he was a popular and forceful speaker. Masters endured his exuberant manner. He may not have been as confident as he appeared, but when on his feet the words flowed and points were made with clarity and pungency. Masters' observations on school reports reflect Heron's developing character:

'Will do well, with a little more steadiness ...'
'Inclines to be frivolous ...'
'Occasional outbursts of exuberance ...'
'Has great intelligence ...'

A lifelong friendship made at Bradford Grammar School was with E.C. Gregory, known as 'Peter', ultimately Chairman of Lund Humphries, who made publishing history with his monographs on such people as Henry Moore, Ben Nicholson and Barbara Hepworth.

In 1906 Heron's form master called on his mother to persuade her to let him sit for a scholarship to Oxford. The form master was told that Tom was going into the family business and he would become a good employer and carry on family tradition. It is difficult to know what would have happened to him had he gone to Oxford. He was a natural student in that he was always anxious to widen and deepen his knowledge, yet he was too much a young man of action to face several years of academic work. And again his mind turned to the subject of work, as he later reflected:

'At the Grammar School I recognised some boys as clever, others as swots, and others again merely as good fellows, but only once during my six years' stay do I remember wondering about the nature of work, though the word must often have been used in one way or another. One day when I was about sixteen one of the masters for whom I had a great respect came bouncing into the room five minutes after the time he was due. The noise subsided at once, for it was evident to all that he was in a terrible rage. To our surprise he was not cross with us for anything we had done. He let off an eloquent tirade against his lot as a schoolmaster, which we were given to understand was an underpaid, overworked profession! Now my father and other businessmen had not failed to point out to me how fortunate schoolmasters were, inasmuch as they were paid for doing nothing all through the long school holidays, so the idea of a schoolmaster being overworked struck me as comical. But this particular master had won my confidence. During a poetry lesson we had giggled at the word 'love', which came in the sonnet we were doing, and he had immediately stopped the lesson to explain to us quite good humouredly that it really was love that made the world go round. So, after hours, I used the holiday argument as a gambit to find out how a schoolmaster could possibly consider himself overworked. In the encounter, my opinion of the business man suffered a shock from which it has never recovered, and years later, when I came across Chaucer's

'No-wher so bisy a man as he ther nas,
And yet he semed bisier than he was.'

I remembered my astonished helplessness before the onslaught of a man who judged work by its intensity and thought it sub-human to value it in terms of money.

This revelation enabled me for the first time to see the link between what I had heard in church Sunday after Sunday, and the affairs of everyday life, and as I was now at an age when I had to make up my mind what I was going to do in life, it undoubtedly contributed to my decision to go into business as my father had done and to hang on to the Church – also as he had done. But now I naturally had some awkward questions to ask about the business I was to enter and I found that many of them were questions which had troubled my mother for years.

It was clear that I had to make money. Otherwise I could not live and bring up a family. It was equally clear that some ways of making money were wrong, and that all the wrong ways were not punishable by law. My mother had been very much impressed by Mr Ruskin's ideas about the righteousness of a profit of ten per cent, and the unrighteousness of any rate which exceeded this. My father had never been able to see any connection between what Mr Ruskin had said and the Bradford trade, and, in any case, he had never been able to make anything like ten per cent profit!'

Edmund Heron was a well known figure in the piece goods section of the Bradford woollen trade. He was in business as a manufacturer's agent and stuff merchant. It was in his father's business that Tom Heron started work as an office boy. He regarded it as an adventure and there was only one point on which he was really clear: that hard work would bring success.

'Alas, my observations during my first few months completely disillusioned me on even this point,' he later commented. 'I noticed that the businessmen who were successful were hardly ever those who worked the hardest! There were plenty of managers and foremen who were applauded as perfect gluttons for work, but the successful Bradford businessmen were those who played dominoes or chess in the cafés, occasionally asking about a price for yarns or a delivery date for piece goods as they prepared for the next game. And the most successful men went shooting or fishing

On holiday: Tom's Father and Mother (seated right) with left–right Aunt Kate, Tom, Kathleen and Winnie.

Edmund and Annie Heron with their family 1913 left to right: Tom, Kathleen, Frank and Winnie.

or took themselves and their wives off to Bournemouth when the March winds came. At first I thought the explanation to be that only the successful businessmen could afford to do these things, but after a year or two I realized that all the men who played dominoes were not wealthy, that some comparatively poor men became wealthy apparently as a result of the domino technique, but that all the domino players did not become wealthy – some of them failed and had to take jobs which left them no time for the cafés.'

This may have been baffling to Heron at the time, but it was another ingredient to add to his developing philosophy of work. Another quickly followed, when the family moved from Bradford to live under the moorland crags at Eastby, near Skipton. He rapidly absorbed all the details of the small village community.

'My first impression of the Dales farmer was that he was always to be found walking down the village street with an empty bucket over his arm and a dog at his heels, or else leaning over a gate looking at his pastures. Of course, he could always find time for a talk, and his talk always fell naturally upon simple subjects connected with his life. He talked well. Compared with his, most townsmen's talk was theoretical and lean. Nearly every farmer had a man and the farmer's man worked but, as I often used to say, the farmer himself was the Lord of Creation, and all God's Creation worked for him. On the other hand, the farmer's wife was undeniably a worker. She prepared his breakfast for him in the morning, took a hand at milking, got the children off to school, kept the house clean, did the baking and the washing, looked after her hens, mended, and in some cases made, the family clothes, did whatever work was done in the garden, made the butter, helped with the haymaking, and took in visitors during summer. In addition, she acted as the family representative at church on Sundays. This division of labour seemed to suit both parties. Divorces were almost unheard of. I began to wish I were a farmer myself, and when I thought of the farmer's wife, I felt a contempt for the middle-class town wife, whose work seemed mostly shopping and bullying servants to do totally unnecessary work. When I went lambing, I realised that the farmer could work hard and for long hours on end when the job required it, and once when an early fall of snow caught the sheep on the moors, I saw a different man at work from the philosopher who had leaned over the gateway – the intensity about which my schoolmaster had spoken was inherent in the farmer's job as well as in the teacher's. But I did not realise the implications of my observations about rural work until some ten years later when I found myself living in another type of natural community.'

Heron left school in 1906 at the age of sixteen and eagerly entered the man's world in his father's business. There he remained until the end of 1910, by which time he had been open to many other potent influences. He joined the Bradford Debating Society and in 1907 and 1908 was debating such subjects as 'Does Capital Punishment Deter?' (he thought it did) and 'Should the British Government grant Egypt an independent national status? (he thought it should). He was an avid reader and a commonplace book he kept at the time is full of extracts from the writings of Thomas Carlyle, Edward Carpenter, John Ruskin and, above all, Walt Whitman, who, with Tolstoy, were pervading influences.

We shall return to Tom Heron at work, starting his own business and the way in which both religion and politics set him on a path which was to bring him into contact with some of the choicest spirits of the age. But first it is necessary to jump ahead to consider one of the most powerful influences on his development.

Chapter Two

Culture, Causes and Conscience

IN THE FIRST DECADE OF THIS CENTURY there were many radical movements in thought, literature, art, politics, philosophy and much else. That they should find a locus in a place as unlikely as that of Leeds, was for Heron, as for countless others, a life-enhancing jolt, administered principally by the Leeds Arts Club founded in 1902 by Alfred Richard Orage. Both the Club and its founder were to have an immediate and lasting effect on Heron.

Orage was a brilliant man of letters, an important publicist and a literary critic. Though largely self-educated, he was a student of Plato, Plotinus and the wisdom of the East. Unconventional and emancipated in what was still a stuffy and claustrophobic age, he was among the first to acclaim the discoveries of Freud and Jung. Aphorisms, profundities and subtleties flowed from the pen of this man, whom Bernard Shaw called 'a desperado of genius.' He couldn't help irritating, even infuriating, people besides influencing them. When he died in 1934, T.S. Eliot paid tribute to him:

'Many people will remember Orage as the tireless and wholly disinterested evangelist of monetary reform; many will remember him as the best leader-writer in London – on Wednesday mornings I always read through the first part of the *New English Weekly* before attending to any other work. A smaller number will remember him, as R.H.C. of *The New Age*, as the best literary critic of that time in London. Some will remember him as the benevolent editor who encouraged merit and (what is rarer) tolerated genius. He was something more than the sum of these. He was a man who could be both perfectly right and wholly wrong; but when he was wrong one respected him all the more, as a man who was seeking the essential things and therefore was unafraid of making a fool of himself – a very rare quality indeed. What was great about him was not his intelligence, fine as that was, but his honesty and his selflessness. Most of us have not the self-knowledge to realise how parasitic we are upon the few men of fixed principle and selfless devotion, how the pattern of our world depends, not so much upon what they teach us, but just upon their being there.' (*New English Weekly*, 15 November 1934)

Many of the most creative talents of the period replied to the question, 'Where were you educated?' by saying, 'In the pages of *The New Age*.' It is easy to see what Heron admired in Orage. He too was naturally attracted to ideas and if they were expressed in a magnetically compulsive and imaginative manner, he was easily – sometimes too easily – drawn and hooked!

Another founding member of the Leeds Arts Club also influenced Heron. Arthur

J. Penty was a Leeds architect. Born in 1875, he showed considerable academic promise but was removed from school at the age of thirteen by his father, to be apprenticed as an architect. Success came early and he was the designer of several buildings in York while still in his late teens. But at the age of twenty-one, in 1896, Penty suddenly realised his lack of education and began to read, particularly history. As an architect in sympathy with the Arts and Crafts movement, it was not surprising that he would turn to Ruskin and Morris. By 1897 he considered himself a Socialist and in rapid succession joined the York Fabian Society and the Independent Labour Party. He also joined the Theosophical Society, more in order to make contact with wider outlooks than his own than through belief in its doctrines. And that is where Penty met Orage.

During his training as an architect, Penty saw many examples of 'commercial intrigue and speculation' and became unhappy with his continued association with his father's firm. An interest in medieval architecture (he compared it with that of his own period, which was found wanting) led Penty to Ruskin, and in Ruskin he found the idea of restoring guilds, and, in so doing, restoring the traditional arts and crafts.

Orage and Penty spent long hours together discussing the 'Restoration of the Guild System' (which was to be the title of Penty's key work, published in 1906). They had not only idealistic aims, but also extravagant ambitions to transform the culture of Leeds and ultimately that of the whole country. Club meetings were addressed by such people as Edward Carpenter, G.K.Chesterton, Bernard Shaw and Orage himself. They had one characteristic in common: all were enthusiasts.

Although Heron had heard of the Leeds Arts Club as early as 1906, and had regretted that he had missed a lecture by Edward Carpenter on Walt Whitman (for Heron was a keen Whitmanite), he did not become a member until 1911. From then until his departure for Cornwall in 1924, he became a regular attender at meetings.

Orage had left Leeds for London in 1907 to edit the *New Age* and, according to Heron, the tone at the Leeds Arts Club had dropped a bit by the time he joined.

'And then suddenly Sir Michael Sadler was appointed to the Vice Chancellorship of Leeds University and Frank Rutter was appointed to be curator of the Art Gallery and those two brought an absolute new lease of life.'

Sadler's buoyant manner and creative enthusiasm were infectious and Heron quickly came under his influence, not least at the monthly meetings which Sadler held at his home and which were open to members of the Arts Club. These were lively, serious, argumentative and enriching evenings, where particular paintings were discussed or an artist's work appraised in his presence. The paintings in Sadler's collection were a revelation in themselves, including, as it did, works by Kandinski and Klee, as well as those of Post-Impressionists such as Gaughin and Van Gogh. Among the artists invited to Sadler's and the Club were Paul and John Nash, Harold Gilman, Stanley and Gilbert Spencer and C.R.W. Nevinson. The Leeds

Tom Heron by Bruce Turner c.1916.

painters Bruce Turner and Jacob Kramer were already members of the Club. Both were friends of Heron's and painted striking portraits of him. Heron long remembered the paintings, the artists and the members' discussions:

'It was while discussing one of these new pictures that I first met Herbert Read, who silently crept in while he was a student at Leeds University and listened to the discussion.'

So began another long friendship, between two men who searched with a common integrity and intensity but were separated by widely differing talents and dispositions. Heron was to comment on Read in a BBC programme in 1977:

'In a curious way I think the army discipline suited something in his nature. There was none of the anarchist about him as far as army orders were concerned. He liked the tidiness of it. And he accused me of being a Christian anarchist, saying that I only believed in obeying the laws of the land when I approved of them.'

A vivid picture of the Leeds Arts Club at that time and of the rôle of Frank Rutter, its new President, is to be found in David Thistlewood's publication, *Herbert Read, Formlessness and Form, An Introduction to his Aesthetics*.

'He brought from London an aesthetic hypothesis, a theory of 'significant form', maintaining that it was form itself – lines, shapes, colours, irrespective of pictorial content – which stimulated aesthetic emotion during contemplation of works of art. Club members had for several years insisted on the primacy of quick, expressive sketches over finished drawings and paintings. Rutter now urged that such sketches need not necessarily be pictorial, and he encouraged attempts to represent musical sound and composition by means of reflex painting, and to correlate words with drawings representing nothing other than emotions which the words aroused.'

Emphasizing the importance of the Club to Read, Thistlewood comments:

'It was at the Leeds Arts Club that the village schoolboy, the orphanage pupil, the night school student, the student of economics, gained his most effective and unlikely education.'

The experiments Rutter instigated were remembered with relish by Heron long after they took place:

'A talented local pianist played six tunes and eight or nine of us sketched the movements on large sheets of paper, after which we shuffled our efforts and spread them out on the floor. On about the third occasion we all spotted the 'Sheep may Safely Graze' and Rachmaninoff's Prelude. But our efforts to produce coloured abstracts of Bach and Mozart failed miserably, although Bruce Turner (an artist) was concerned that each note on an organ had its appropriate colour and told us about the American instrument which played all sorts of coloured lights.'

When members of the Leeds Arts Club were enthusing about the impressionists, a noted photographer and member of the Leeds Photographic Society accused them of painting lies instead of what they really saw. Heron was amongst those who accepted the challenge. He, with some other members of the Club, arranged a tripod in a garden at Headingley so that any camera placed upon it had to focus on an assortment of distant and near objects, ranging from a spray of leaves almost touching it to distant hills and mill chimneys. A sunny Sunday afternoon was chosen for the experiment on what proved to be a smokeless day. The Photographic Society was challenged to get ten or twelve of its members to photograph the view and attend the next meeting of the Arts Club with enlargements of an agreed size which could be compared. They undertook not to show one another their photographs until the Club meeting. The result was fascinating for the Club and devastating for the Society. As much as twenty per cent difference occurred in the proportions of the measurement of the height and length of a deceptively square building in the middle ground, while a tall slim tree trunk a yard or so in front of the camera, which divided the view exactly into two, appeared to be made of different substances. Thereafter there was a rewarding respect, if healthy tension, between Society and Club members.

It is not difficult to see that Heron's eyes would be prized open and his mind stretched in this company. He learned that the enemy of art (as of religion) is the belief that the intellect can understand all. These artists increased his range of vision. Once shaken out of his prejudices or ignorance, and constantly buffeted so that he could never think the same way again, Heron now had an artistic instinct for life. Years later he spoke of his experience:

'I began to take Art seriously as a result of a chance meeting with a painter at the Leeds Arts Club. Somehow I felt that both in his life and in his work he was expressing certain values about which, as it were, I only knew by hearsay. On a great many matters I knew instinctively that I was wiser than he was, and indeed it was because he was trusting me implicitly to help him in certain ways that I was able to trust him with equal certainty in others ... I was fortunate in finding one who quickly dashed each hard-won certainty as soon as I came by it. One day everything would depend upon the significant line which was the painter's answer to the dread injunction, 'Give it a name;' the next day I would be told that there were no lines in nature, only light. Logic was used in scraps and patches, surely its true mode of application; laws were invented to fit the experience; eventually, "if you really find it to be so, it must be so" made one realise that it was much more important to get rid of bad principles than to rely on good ones.'

In 1959, when the St Anne's Society in London was proposing to have an evening devoted to painting, Heron sent a memorandum to his fellow Council members which opened thus:

'The painter's function may be said to be that of increasing the visual sensitivity and awareness of those who look at his paintings. When, as is usually the case, he has to sell his work in order to live, he has in every age to put up with the fact that most of his potential patrons are not at all interested in having their visual awareness extended. What they want is something which will give them pleasure and symbolize their status and achievement. But the true painter, whilst giving them what they think they want, always manages to add something personal to himself. This personal contribution – the painter's style – has the effect of giving a new interpretation to the 'subject', and does so by affecting us at a deeper level of consciousness than reason alone reaches. It is this process which has enabled artists in every age to civilize the up-and-coming ruling class (the class which has the time and money to spend on art) and, by so doing, to make them dissatisfied with the crude ideas about power, wealth, birth, manners or cleverness which have raised them to power.'

Heron, the young businessman, was from the start a patron of the 'avant garde' and, as his son, the influential artist Patrick Heron, has noted, 'in 1911 that phrase was a potent one.'

The majority of members of Leeds Arts Club supported the suffragettes in their aspirations and campaigning. Heron's involvement is best described in extracts from letters written to his future wife. We see him challenged by a suffragette in November 1912:

'I stayed in Leeds and popped in to a Militant Suffrage meeting at which Frank Rutter was speaking. I was asked to join in and did so willingly. Mrs Cohen, a well-known suffragette, was there. She is an out-and-out militant and a wonderfully gentle, mature woman. She it was who had a smashing whack at the Crown Jewels. I liked her immensely. She has a wonderfully sad wistful face and eyes. She asked me why I was not doing more for the women. I had a long talk with her and found her able to understand and appreciate my objections to militancy. However she got me to speak for them and yesterday I had two rousing meetings. One in the Miners' Institute and the other – Praise the Lord! – in Town Hall Square (Leeds) on Sunday night. We had a great time with the crowd. Plenty of policemen and detectives. We quietened the roughs and let fly at the Government. I told the workers that their revolt was the women's revolt, that the governing classes had entrenched themselves behind certain privileges and until we cleared them out, men would not be able to live the wonderful lives they are capable of. I said that women had at length realised what womanhood and motherhood meant and that it was this vision which made them want to smash away the inequalities and prejudices which fettered them.'

When Heron stated that he was opposed to militancy, what did he mean, and why?

'First, because it is inexpedient. The Govt. can always squash you with the Police and the Army. Secondly, because at present at any rate we must have laws, otherwise the individual would not have the liberty of action and thought protected. Under a democracy, I would be a stickler for 'Loranorder', as the *Herald* calls it. I would say that if the minority does not like a law, it will have to educate the rest of the community until they find themselves in the majority. Progress consists of the education of majorities by minorities. As far as the women are concerned, the second reason does not apply. They are outside the constitution and not morally bound by any of the laws.

'I always oppose Militancy in their case on the grounds of expediency. It does not pay. Men who have votes ought to use them properly and deserve to suffer if they don't like the laws they have made. The Militants have asked me to speak for them because I attack the Government and insist on it that the Govt. is responsible for all this trouble. There would never have been any militancy if the Government had handled this agitation in a thoroughly democratic manner. I believe I have managed to prevent attempts at burnings and window-smashing. I want the women to agitate and I believe I am getting them to do it as it has never been done in Leeds before. Meetings in Town Hall Square every night and one on Woodhouse Moor tomorrow. I have spoken four times this week. I am getting run down and shall be ready for Whitsuntide. Half my energy goes now in restraining myself, but I am certain that a man who is always in a position to let himself go is a poor agitator.' (Letter, March 1913)

On several occasions Heron was interviewed by the Chief Constable of Leeds. The meetings were friendly but the advice was clear. Heron would be well advised to cease his campaigning. Naturally, it was an invitation easy to decline. But Heron's support for the suffrage movement did not stop at addressing and haranguing the public. He was involved, with other members of the Arts Club, in two escapes. In the Autumn of 1914 a noted suffragette, Lilian Lenten, had set fire to the pavilion in Richmond Park. She was caught, sentenced to prison and went on hunger strike. She was released under the 'Cat and Mouse' Act but escaped, travelled to Yorkshire, set fire to another building, was caught and sentenced again. She was serving her sentence in Armley Jail when Club members heard of her plight through a friend of hers, Nora Duval, who had travelled to Leeds to organise the escape. The plan began when Lilian Lenten went on hunger strike and Heron takes up the story:

'Frank Rutter's wife was a keen suffragist so it was decided that her name should be submitted to the police as a suitable person to house Lilian when the prison doctors said her life would be endangered if she was kept in prison any longer. Under the Act all that Mrs Rutter had to do was to promise to let the prison doctor come and examine the patient after a fortnight had elapsed. It happened that the driver of Reynold and Branson's horse-drawn delivery cart was a keen suffragist. So it was arranged that Nora Duval, who was very much Lilian's build, should dress up as a grocer's boy and be ready to go up with the cart and deliver a big basket of soda water syphons and other medicaments and delicacies, immediately the prison authorities told Mrs Rutter to expect Lilian. Our doctor, (a Club member) and a nurse were also waiting for the signal to go to Rutter's house. The idea was that Lilian should be dressed in a similar outfit to the grocer's boy, that when Nora Duval knocked at the back and said, 'Reynold and Branson', Mrs Rutter should say the basket was too heavy

Edmund, Annie, Kathleen and Tom at Eastby Hall.

for her to lift and ask the 'boy' to bring it in. After the 'boy' had emptied the load onto the kitchen table, the new boy, Lilian, should take the empty basket out, get on the cart with it and be driven to the end of the street, where I was waiting with a motor car to take her to a sympathiser's house in Harrogate. I had been chosen for this task because although the police knew I was a sympathiser, they also knew I had spoken against the violent tactics and on one occasion had persuaded two nice old ladies to pour down the sink the gun powder they had been given to make pillar box incendiary bombs. Lilian went gaily past the two policemen at the back door but collapsed as she was trying to get on to the cart. Somehow we got her into the car and I drove off to Harrogate, convinced that the police had seen what had happened and would be on our trail. It meant going to Scarborough, not Harrogate. However, on my return to Leeds, the police were still guarding the house. As previously arranged, visitors were calling with flowers and the doctor made his daily visit. You can imagine the uproar when, on the expiration of the fortnight, the prison doctor was allowed in and found that the bird had flown. Frank Rutter's passive part in the escapade cost him his job.'

The second escape involved some twenty club members. The ultimate venue was a house in Harrogate and the escape was arranged the day before the prison doctor was to visit the house. A dance was arranged at the club and members dressed themselves as ghosts, using white sheets for the purpose. At a pre-arranged time the dancers marched – or rather glided – out of the club to the railway station in Leeds and boarded a train for Harrogate. On arrival, these versatile ghosts sang their way to the house and entered by the back door one by one, with two policemen trying to peer in each face; then by a circuitous route they emerged from the front door. This was done two or three times. Then they separated in groups of three, dispersed over the Stray, a large open park, removed their hoods and sheets and made for waiting cars. As all their faces had been covered by white hoods with holes for eyes, the police were helpless and did not realize that the ghosts had multiplied during the escapade.

Heron was still actively involved in 1915:

'Today I have had to go up to the Civil Court to give evidence at Mrs Cohen's trial. She was arrested on Sunday night and cast into the cells with drunkards etc. The prosecution rooted up some of my old speeches when I was in the witness box, but I managed to explain them. Great excitement here.'

It was not all and always unity of action at the Club. When the First World War came, there were deep cleavages. Some were eager to fight; others, not eager to enlist, succumbed to populist agitation; others were conscientious objectors. Heron had discussed this with many people, not least Ben Keeling, with whom he shared lodgings in Leeds for a time. F.H. 'Ben' Keeling had been a Wykehamist, history scholar of Trinity College, Cambridge, and the acknowledged leader of Cambridge undergraduate Socialism. An impetuous iconoclast, he was a rather rough type, with a tendency to violence of thought and expression. He was a dominating person with immense vitality and great fun as a friend. But his conscience tortured him. H.G. Wells described him as 'a copious, rebellious, disorderly, generous and sympathetic young man'. It is not difficult to imagine the earnest arguments which took place between Heron and Keeling, a bracing wind rather than hot air. It was Keeling who prodded Heron in the direction of The Fabian Society and the Independent Labour Party. They seemed to agree on pacifism.

But for Heron it had not always been thus. At seventeen he had joined the Territorial Army, seeing it in terms of glamour, comradeship and adventure.

'From 1907 to 1910 I drilled and went to their camps for a fortnight each year and I had my red coat and my khaki trews and I enjoyed getting dirty climbing up hillsides on my tummy and all that kind of thing.'

In April 1910, away in Belgium, his sister Kathleen heard all about it. 'Tom is one of the best shots in his company,' wrote his other sister Winnie, 'You ought to be proud of him!' She and their mother had attended a church parade that Sunday to see Tom in his finery. The maternal comment by the same post confirmed that Tom and a friend 'had managed to infect me with a little enthusiasm re soldiering.' Clearly she had no military ambition for her second son. On the other hand, her positive contribution to the development of his pacifist convictions was unlikely to have amounted to much more than the independence of mind he had inherited from her, which some labelled 'free thinking'.

In later years, while recognising the influence of Tolstoy, Heron always attributed his exchanging juvenile playing at soldiers for unshakeable pacifism to Norman Angel's book, *The Great Illusion*, which appeared in 1910. 'I read it with great excitement and then I started propaganding for it', speaking frequently in its defence in public. Without doubt Angel's argument convinced Heron intellectually but the ground was ready for the seed of other influences which were to follow.

The 'Great War' did not come as a bolt from the blue. The possibility of conflict, even its likelihood, had long provoked civilian debate. While peace lasted, anti-war views were often aired, particularly at gatherings of the Fabians, the I.L.P. and the Leeds Arts Club, all frequented by Heron. Even after war began, many of his closest friends stuck to their pacificism, notably the Davies family into which he was to marry before peace returned. Heron's pacifism was all of a piece (to borrow a textile phrase) with the rest of his philosophy, which became increasingly organic and conservationist as the years passed. But it was the pacifism that led to the conservation not the other way round, while both sprang from his basic religious sense of the duty of man towards God's creation. For Heron the influences of intellect, religion and friendship converged.

It was not only the mindless conduct of the campaigns across the Channel that confirmed his opposition to war. So too did his involvement in the suffragette struggle, which gave him experience of non-violence in action.

The pacifist case, which was inevitably muffled once war began, gained a new lease of life with the introduction of conscription in January 1916. By that time Heron's mind had long been made up.

The fact that he, the ex-Territorial, was known as a protagonist of pacifism for five years before conscription was introduced accounts in part for his being granted unconditional exemption. His personal statement on that occasion, which shows how deeply pacifism had taken root, deserves to be quoted in full:

'I have a conscientious objection to War and under no circumstance will I bear arms. During the last 5 or 6 years this objection has been growing and deepening. Now it dominates my whole being.

'Every part of my nature cries out against this orgy of bloodshed and hatred. Every one of my senses forbids me to take part in it. My intellect tells me that war is inefficient. It never achieves what it sets out to achieve.

'My emotions find it a degrading activity, not one which uplifts and refines.

'In my Religion there is no place for it. I believe in constructive work, not destructive. I believe in the sacredness of human life, not the commonness of it. I believe in reasoning about a difference, not fighting about it. I believe in trying to understand those who differ from me, not killing them. I believe in loving my enemies, not hating them. I believe in the oneness of humanity, not in the separateness of the nations.

'Probably more than 90% of the soldiers engaged on both sides in this war believe that they are fighting in defence of their hearths and homes. No combatant nation would continue the struggle for a single day longer, were it not convinced that its enemy was the aggressor. There must, then, be a misconception somewhere, and misconceptions cannot be blasted away by cannon shot or dispersed at the point of a bayonet. They can only be removed by fearless reasoning and by the display of a genuine desire to understand and help.

'I cannot go out to slap people who are fighting because they do not understand me or my country. My way of serving my country at this juncture must be by doing what little is in my power to find out how the legitimate aims and ideals of the British peoples and their Allies can be pursued by them without interfering with the legitimate aims and ideals of the German races. My faith tells me that there is need in the World for the 'best' of both races; my philosophy, that their 'worst' can only be eliminated by their 'best'.

'Satan cannot cast out Sin, neither can Militarists cast out militarism. Prussian Militarism, or any other Militarism, can only be destroyed by the people themselves, when they have learnt that they have no further need for it. Defeat them in battle and you only convince them that their warlike preparations were not on a large enough scale. They will rearm at the first opportunity.

'The only way to prevent war is to create an international conscience which will refuse to tolerate it. Formerly family used to wage war against family, and city against city. The growth of a public, and a national, conscience has made that a thing of the past. I desire to work for the growth of an international relationship which will bring us one step nearer universal peace.

'I am engaged in work which is constructive. I desire to be allowed to pursue it. I cannot take the Military oath, for that would deprive me of my freedom. I am responsible unto God for my conduct and must be free to act, at all times, as my conscience dictates, for that is the only way I can be of any use to humanity.'

Chapter Three

Modern Medievalist

FOUR YEARS' BUYING AND SELLING CLOTH for his father's agency introduced Heron to a wide section of the textile industry and left him confident of his powers as a salesman. It was inevitable that he would want to have his own business. He was too self-assertive and self-reliant to remain an employee of his father, whatever the future appeared to hold in terms of promotion prospects and security. He did not want security. He wanted independence. In a 1912 letter he wrote: 'Some children (they say) don't want to grow up. I always wanted to be at the height of my manhood.'

On January 3rd, 1911, the first day the law allowed, being his twenty-first birthday, he went into partnership with a friend, Bob Wilkinson, who was already manufacturing blouses in Meanwood Road, Leeds. Though they began to prosper, they soon realized they were too similar in temperament to forge themselves into an effective team and parted that July on amicable terms. In spite of having only six months' experience as a manufacturer, Heron immediately set up his own blouse-making business, specializing in delaines, taffetas and silks. He obtained premises in 68 East St., Leeds, moving into an empty factory that had been a flax mill. In July 1912 the audited accounts showed a net profit of £60 after taking into account payments of thirty shillings a week to himself and the cost of his first-class rail pass from Bradford to Leeds. Progress would have been slow with so little capital, had it not been for his uncle Joshua Milner, who was engaged in a profitable shirt-manufacturing business. He was a Tory straight and true but he had watched his nephew's career with interest and was impressed, so when he quarrelled with his partner, he made what Heron regarded as 'an astounding offer', to come into partnership with him, bringing £6,000 capital. In 1913 they established the T.M. Heron Company Ltd. (the title itself broke with convention), with its factory, the Springwell Works, in Buslingthorpe Lane, Leeds. They became joint managing directors, drawing equal salaries of £1,500 a year. Milner was in charge of the accounts and costings whilst Heron's innovative energies were devoted to design, buying and selling. The Company notepaper was aquamarine with herons in flight across the title and address. Heron's originality was also seen in the trade mark, 'Miona', which was sown into all the blouses the company made. At that time the use of such tabs was limited to advertising well-known retailers, but not manufacturers.

The outbreak of war in 1914 had surprisingly little immediate effect on the fortunes of the T.M. Heron Company, which continued to build on its promising foundations in spite of Heron's refusal to accept what was known as 'war work,' such as the Government contracts to supply the forces, which kept many firms afloat. Throughout the war, his business involved Heron in one or two trips a month to London, where he found time to see most of the avant-garde exhibitions and spend many evenings at the Café Royal, where Orage gathered round himself a stimulating court of writers, thinkers and artists.

For the moment we shall turn from Heron's business life to dramatic developments in his philosophy and the ideas and ideals which impressed themselves on everything he did.

Keeping the company he kept and reading the books he read, it was inevitable that Heron would devote time and talents to politics and for him that meant socialism. He was never seduced by the revolutionary aspect of socialism, represented in the British Socialist Party, which derived its main inspiration from the teachings of Marx. He saw the appeal of the Independent Labour Party, which represented the more moderate school and was evolutionary in tendency, displaying a readiness to unite itself with other 'progressive' forces. An audience listening to Heron's fiery speeches for the Independent Labour Party might have been forgiven for wondering if he was advocating revolution. He wasn't, but his rhetoric, with colourful allusions, roused people. It was only on reflection that they realized that here was no political spouting with cliché or bombast, but a real radical with some unusual ideas.

Heron also joined the Fabian Society, a middle-class body, which not only aimed at the study of socialist problems, but also sought to permeate men of all parties with socialist ideas. Heron became a frequent attender and regular debater and speaker at Fabian gatherings, and until his marriage, went each year to the Fabian Summer School.

Much as he was drawn to ideas, Heron was more attracted to the people behind them. So he was drawn to an individualist like William Morris (1834–1896). Morris's revolt against the false and narrow aims of industrialism, his preaching of the need for freedom in labour and joy in the performance of it, his insistence upon the vital nature of human fellowship and the need for a world which should value beauty rather than riches, were in Heron's eyes one of the greatest contributions made in England to the socialist idea.

Socialism was more than a political philosophy to Heron at this time. He shed regular church-going when he left his parents' home to live in Leeds during the war. His belief in God had not been similarly discarded but had been put into cold storage for a time – or so he thought.

'Socialism is the New Religion, or rather the old religion expressed in terms which we moderns can appreciate,' he wrote in a letter to his future wife in 1913. 'The Political Socialist Movement, in spite of its narrowness and petty bigotry, is really a live movement and I cling to it for it enables me to translate my religion into terms of political science. In a way, to become a Socialist means to be born again. One sees Art, Work, Motherhood, Fatherhood, Worship, Play ... all in a new light. A new vision of life is revealed and if anyone is young and strong and healthy, one longs to do something to make the vision a reality. I don't care a rap which way a man chooses to work. All I care about is that he should see the Ideal.'

It may appear that the gushing nature of the language suggests an uncritical commitment to the socialist cause. That was not quite the case. Heron usually wrote and spoke with unbridled, but not unconsidered, force. About this time he was agonizing about his work and his politics.

'Bob and I talked about "losing our souls" working in a town. We both feel our businesses do us a tremendous lot of harm ... I get to hate my factory more & more, yet I am more & more drawn to the people in it and about it ... I'm what you may call a working Socialist and the business is just a stage in my career.'

He did not rule out a career in politics – indeed he half expected his career would lead him that way. However a movement was emerging which united his political convictions with his developing ideas about the nature of work. Later, religion acted as a catalyst to give substance and form to it.

The 'movement' led to the formation of the National Guilds League. The restoration of the word 'guild' as a challenge to modern capitalism and to most of the prevalent remedies for it, was largely due to A.J. Penty. Penty, with Orage and Samuel G. Hobson, are usually regarded as the fathers of Guild Socialism. From his experience as an architect, and in attempting to find a market for the product of modern craftsmanship, Penty came to the conclusion – reinforced by his discontent with the palliatives of the Fabian Society propaganda – that for the cure of modern industrialism, something much more fundamental was needed than the collectivist and bureaucratic ideas then prevalent among British Socialists. His book, *The Restoration of the Gild System** had great influence on Heron. He admired the independence and originality of Penty and appreciated the value and significance of medieval civilization, whilst being blind to some of its evils. Penty's demand was in substance a bold plea for the subordination of industrialism to craftsmanship and a return to the old localized civilization of which the guilds were an essential part. But stated in this form, the Guild idea did not appear to have any very immediate application to the industrial issues in which Heron was immersed and about which he had strong views. It was Orage who, with some fellow writers and contributors to *The New Age*, began to formulate the doctrine of National Guilds. These writers attacked the central bastion of capitalism – the Wage System. In its place there would be Guild Socialism, which was an ingenious synthesis of political Socialism and industrial Syndicalism. The Trade Unions were to be converted into Guilds, which, by virtue of their 'monopoly of labour', could demand that the State should give them control of industries and services. (Ideally clerical and administrative workers other than directors would be members of the guilds presenting this demand.) Both shareholders and the State would be helpless in the face

---

* NB. Penty had a fad about spelling the word "GILD" – which is why the published title of his work has GILD not GUILD.

of this concerted action. The State would purchase each industry and issue its Guild a charter stating the conditions under which it would be allowed to operate. Its responsibilities would include the maintainance of high standards of quality and a fixed price for its products (to be determined by a joint body representing all Guilds and the State); the Guild would pay a single tax or rent to the State (determined by the same body). Factories would be locally controlled – a Guild consisting of all the factories in a particular type of industry. Each Guild member would be assured of continuous pay, full medical coverage and a pension; the Government would not be burdened with the administration of these social services. The early Guild Socialists did not envisage the disappearance of the State, as did the Syndicalists; the citizens as a whole would elect a Government which would regulate the Guilds, enact national legislation and conduct international affairs. But they were opposed to the gargantuan bureaucracy of Fabian Socialism, with its omnipotent centralization of power. The basic premise of the movement, according to G.D.H. Cole, was that:

'men could not be really free as citizens unless they were also free and self-governing in their daily lives as producers.'

The motto of the movement was taken from the Apocrypha:

'They shall maintain the fabric of the world, and in the handywork of their craft is their prayer.'

It was the ethical emphasis of Guild Socialism which made it attractive to a wide range of people. The National Guilds League was founded in 1915. G.D.H. Cole and Maurice Reckitt were influential figures in its formation. Cole, the unapproachable, cold atheist – and at root an anarchist – joined forces with Reckitt, the clubbable, romantic medievalist, archetypal bourgeois and unswerving Anglican with a dogmatic faith, to found the League. Its objects were:

'The abolition of the Wage System and the establishment of Self-Government in Industry through a system of National Guilds working in conjunction with the State.'

The forty men and women who met in April 1915 to set up the National Guilds League were a fascinating and attractive mixture in age, thought and experience. This was part of the initial force and promise of the group. But it carried the seeds of the League's demise for there were too many dissimilarities in background and conviction. They spanned different generations. The political experience of the older generation had commenced in the 1880's and 1890's – perhaps even earlier. Emily Townsend had, as a young woman, campaigned for John Stuart Mill. Others, such as George Lansbury and P.E.T. Widdrington, had, like Orage and Hobson, been active in the Socialist and Labour movements in the 1890's. The younger generation were only beginning their political lives. Many had joined the Fabian Society in the wake of H.G. Wells and were, in general, university educated. Ideological differences cut across those of education and generation. Some Guilds even saw themselves as Socialists first and foremost and believed the Guild idea to be the best means for the organization of a Socialist society. Others considered that socialism was discredited by Fabianism and the Labour Party. The Guild idea in this view was a substitiute for socialism and not its means of realization. Again some identified strongly with the Church of England and belonged to the Church Socialist League. Others identified themselves more closely with the Labour movement and the Independent Labour Party.

Historians such as Dr Jack Vowles point out that the Guild movement was formed round two poles. 'As a part of the literary world of London, the *New Age* had a different outlook on matters of theory from that of the university Socialists.' To these contrasting tendencies, the imaginative and the scholarly, a third may be mentioned, for the dimension of the Church was also important. There were, however, significant gaps in its founding membership, notably trade unionists and working managers.

From the outset, the work of the National Guilds League was undertaken in the face of great difficulties. Formed in the midst of war, which necessarily absorbed an increasing share of those who became, or might otherwise have become, its members; with the scantiest of funds; without offices of its own; with its principle organizers busy with multifarious activities in other spheres of the Labour Movement and outside; with the natural suspicion of the trade unions at being 'lectured' from outside to be encountered and overcome, in the face of all these difficulties – the National Guilds League performed a remarkable task.

Enthusiasm for the League strengthened Heron's relations with Cole, whose acquaintance he had made at the Café Royal. Fellow Guild Socialists, Fabians and members of the I.L.P., they were natural colleagues. Cole became a welcome visitor at the Herons' family home at Eastby. Heron dined most uncomfortably with Cole at Magdalen College Oxford, squeezed into a borrowed evening suit, when invited to address the Oxford Socialist Society which Cole had founded – and which Tal Davies, Heron's future brother-in-law, had joined.

Heron joined the League, attended its meetings and was fervent in his support of its ideals. 'Fervent' is an appropriate word to use, for Heron was never lukewarm or half-hearted towards the causes he made his own.

Heron's position during the latter part of the war was unusual. It was not expected that a factory owner-manager would be either a socialist or a pacifist. Heron was both. The longer war went on, the more serious became the rise of inflation and the demand for higher wages. As trade union membership soared, Heron campaigned vigorously for the creation of an official Trade Board, which would include his blouse-makers under its umbrella. Consequently he became chairman of the West Riding Women's Light Clothing Manufacturers Association and for a few years he was on the Trade Board once it was set up. As manager of a factory employing some two hundred people, he could have claimed exemption from conscription. Instead he chose to register as a Conscientious Objector. Moreover, despite the unpopularity and even danger incurred, he refused to hide his pacifism under a

Eulalie Davies and siblings c.1912
Left to Right: Leila, Eulalie, Marjorie, Tal, Kathleen and Lalage.

The Rev. Michael and Annie Davies with their children c.1903
left to right: Tal, Eulalie, Marjorie (standing), Kathleen, Leila and Lalage.

bushel, visiting fellow C.O.s who were in prison not only in Leeds' own Armley Gaol but in Wakefield, Aldershot, Dartmoor and Wormwood Scrubs as well. This experience led him to more general prison visiting after the war.

Heron's pacifism also linked him with Eulalie Davies, whom he married in September 1918, after a long, erratic and turbulent courtship. Known to most people as 'Jack', shortened from 'Jackaboy,' she was the third of five variously gifted daughters of a Congregational minister in Bradford with only one son. It was a claustrophobic household of Brontë-esque passion, ruled by a brilliant but difficult man, whose pro-Boer sympathies led him to forbid his children to stand for the National Anthem sung at school each morning during the Boer War. Under his influence, business was rather despised and the wider world was ignored unless events were mentioned and interpreted in the weekly *Christian World*, for no daily newspaper entered the house. Eulalie never read a newspaper until she went to college at Birmingham. Yet out of this stifling enclosure some brilliant minds emerged.

When it came to marrying, Heron and Eulalie felt they wanted some form of religious service but she had shed her churchgoing when she went to Birmingham in 1911 and he, since leaving home, was a lapsed Presbyterian, partly because of his pacifism. They were much in sympathy with the Quakers because of their stand against warfare, so they arranged to be married at a Friends Meeting House. Heron never forgot how his pacifist campaigning upset their wedding plans.

> 'I was going to be married at the Friends Meeting House in Skipton but three or four days before, we had got Rodan Buxton down to speak for peace by negotiations. He and I spoke from a lorry in the market place, both I think reasoned addresses to stop the carnage and get talking, but at the end of it there was almost a riot.'

Police protection was needed for them to get away safely and because of the hostility aroused in Skipton, the wedding had to be moved at the last minute to the Friends Meeting House in Leeds.

However they soon refrained from attending Quaker meetings. Heron did not feel the Quakers shared his social interests. Nothing was cutting into his soul. Yet he and Eulalie were restless and no longer felt happy with a churchless Sunday. Prior to his marriage, Heron had been lodging for two years with the two Misses Gissing, sisters of George Gissing. They were very devout and spiritual ladies, whose prayer and devotion led to many unadvertised good works. Later Reckitt was to recall the silent influence of the sisters on himself – far more effective than earnest and challenging proselytizing. The Gissing sisters had introduced Heron to one of the Mirfield Fathers. The House of the Resurrection at Mirfield is not far from Leeds and some of the brethren of the Community, such as Father Paul Bull and Father Hilary Jeayes, were active in the Socialist cause.

After marriage, the Herons moved into a house in Far Headingley on the outskirts of Leeds and near to St Chad's Church. They attended occasionally rather than regularly, but it is clear a transformation was taking place. A few years later, when their son Patrick attended and was asked why he liked church, he replied promptly: 'There's lots of music and lots of gold.' And music, colour and atmosphere attracted Heron too. The ordered ritual, reasoned theological sermons and atmosphere of reverence were far removed from extempore prayer and nonconformist worship. The Vicar visited them and explained the doctrine of the Church and the meaning of Anglicanism. Very soon Eulalie and Tom became Anglicans and their first two children, Patrick and Michael, were baptised at St Chad's (one standing, the other in arms.) Appropriately, the godparents included Miss Ellen Gissing and a Mirfield Father.

Heron joined the Church Socialist League (C.S.L.). The impulse to establish the C.S.L. came out of the industrial North. Nominally open to adherents of every 'school' in the Church of England, its main inspiration undoubtedly came from a Catholic section closely in touch with the aspirations of the industrial movement of the great northern cities and towns. Its founding members were priests, Algernon West and W.E. Moll from Tyneside, together with two who had previously been curates in the same area, Conrad Noel and P.E.T. Widdrington. The forceful and witty Lewis Donaldson of Leicester and Fathers Paul Bull and Samuel Healey of the Community of the Resurrection, Mirfield, were also adherents. Lewis Donaldson produced the confident and uncompromising slogan, 'Christianity is the religion of which Socialism is the practice.'

As the C.S.L. developed, lay people assumed many of the offices, including George Lansbury M.P., Maurice Reckitt, Cecil Edward Chesterton (G.K.'s brother) and Ruth Kenyon.

Basically the C.S.L. was a crusade. Crusades sweep people into their ranks – people like Heron. Its method was defined as being 'to cultivate by the regular use of prayer and the sacraments the life of brotherhood,' and devotional activities were always a primary concern of the League. Reckitt was in the thick of it and edited *The Church Socialist* for four years, but later took a detached look at this former glory. But while devotion and propaganda were fully provided for, the basis of the League was far from satisfactory. It accepted a purely secular social theory far too uncritically and, as Widdrington claimed,

'It contained no reference to the obligation of approaching the study of social questions from the standpoint of Christian theology.'

The League, indeed, was not in the mood for any such thing. It was caught in a wave of social enthusiasm, and on that wave it swept forward into a fervour of propaganda, It could not have been otherwise under the whirlwind progress of Conrad Noel, its first organizing secretary, a man whose name was familiar in every industrial area and in all Independent Labour Party branches.

Through the League, Heron was beginning to meet people who would influence his thought and action for the rest of his life. Maurice Benington Reckitt (1888–1980) was one. Reckitt was a man of extraordinary versatility, sharing with Heron an extremely agile mind. In most other respects the two men were very different.

Reckitt was buttressed by a family fortune. His father was a director of Reckitt's ('Blue') of Hull and never 'went out to work'. Instead, he used his considerable gift of writing and collaborating with others in producing books.

His name will recur frequently, as will that of Philippe Auguste Mairet (1886–1975), who, though not a member of C.S.L., first belongs to this period. This was the closest of friendships; the feeling was mutual. Writing to Heron on 11th November 1960, Mairet recalled:

'It is exactly 42 years ago, to within half an hour or so, since we first met in a Leeds café. Your sister Kathleen was there and Ethel Mairet and Bob Wilkinson; while outside the streets were filled with hilarious and joyful crowds hailing the end of the First World War.'

After the war there was a boom in trade and then a slump. Unemployment, which had been virtually non-existent during the war, rose sharply and even passed the two million mark in June 1921. Manufacturers found there was insufficient money in circulation to purchase the goods they were making. Prices plummeted; silks Heron had bought at sixteen shillings a yard were suddenly worth only six. Sales dwindled, stocks of unsaleable goods piled higher and hands were laid off in many firms. Heron, however, was determined to continue providing work for his blouse-makers. It was largely through Heron's friendship with Eric Busby, a working son of the founder of the Bradford store, Busby's, that he was able to reduce his stock pile. Busby bought thousands of Heron's quality silk blouses and advertised them for sale at low prices. The result was that Busby's made little if any money out of the transaction. Heron lost a great deal of money, but for the moment his excellent team of workers remained in employment.

He pressed his uncle and fellow director to cut out the middlemen and sell direct from factory to shop, even to set up shops of their own. Milner disagreed, believing the crisis to be short-lived, so they parted company. Milner chose to keep the factory and buy Heron out. After two years the business failed and closed.

The next two years were the strangest in Heron's business career, and not just because he was abandoning manufacturing for retailing. Finding himself with a wife and two sons to keep, with capital but no business and surrounded by general economic turmoil, he was prey to the idealism of his latest enthusiasm, Guild Socialism. Since hard-headed business was floundering everywhere, he gave idealism its head. So he planned to form a new business incorporating the principles of the National Guilds League. Thus came into being the 'Company of English Merchants', under which title Heron's first two small suburban shops were started in Manningham Lane, Bradford, and Roundhay Road, Leeds. More money was needed and Reckitt, inspired by the plan to give practical effect to the Guild ideal, happily gave money. When Heron was introduced to Reckitt's mother and explained what he was doing, she doubled her son's figure.

Heron asked his wife's brother, Tal Davies, to join in the venture. It seemed an unlikely invitation as Tal had no business experience and seemed destined for an academic career. He had been at Queen's College, Oxford and was about to sit for his Honours in Mods when he was conscripted, and being a conscientious objector, had spent the next three years doing 'hard labour' in various prisons. Oxford refused to take him back after the war and he spent several years pursuing academic courses elsewhere. Heron admired Tal's intelligence and integrity, which was what he needed in the Company of English Merchants. Tal's great school, college and prison friend Henry Stott, whose father was a successful stockbroker, also joined the Company, looking after the finances.

Guild colleagues encouraged Heron to write a pamphlet on the philosophy behind, and inherent in, the Company of English Merchants. He spent some time at Mirfield, where the combined stimulus of sustained silence and sparkling conversation at meal and other times helped him with his first draft. The pamphlet was generally perceived as one of great interest and distinct originality. He did not believe in bargains; his aim was always the just price; his policy selling for cash only. Nevertheless, it may not have been wise, as Eulalie later asserted, to flaunt his principles so openly.

'They should have been kept for your own private use, for you to test the business by from time to time. As it was, you made a sort of public declaration that 'this business is not as other businesses are.'

In the event the firm lost money. Perhaps it was the wrong time for such a venture when other Guilds were folding. Later Heron recognized that to some extent he was out of his depth:

'The only thing I can say about it is that I learnt something about shopkeeping. I was green about it and I bought my experience.'

In 1923 the Church Socialist League transformed itself, not without opposition, from a politically-minded minority into the League of the Kingdom of God. It retained, however, a strongly anti-plutocratic basis. Heron was an active member and an occasional speaker from the outset. Members included A.R. Vidler and Harold Buxton (later Bishop of Gibraltar). The League's leaders at various times included Widdrington, Reckitt, Ruth Kenyon, V.A. Demant, W.G. Peck, and Henry Slesser. They believed, as did Heron, that the Catholic faith of the Church of England demanded a challenge to the world which should take the form of a repudiation of capitalist plutocracy and the wage system. It stood for a social order in which the means of life subserved the commonweal.

When the League came into being, its leaders were almost entirely without influence in Church circles, but this situation soon altered, partly by the influx of powerful new recruits and partly by the seizing of the opportunities to provide a leadership in the sociological field for which, as had been anticipated, many people were eagerly waiting. The first notable example of this was the invitation to the Anglo-Catholic Summer School of Sociology in 1925, in which the League of the Kingdom of God played a leading part.

Heron was a speaker at the first Conference, as he was to be at many others in the future. He made a deep impression by the union of Christian ideals and practical experience which was evident in all he said. It was the theme thought out at Mirfield and subsequently published in *Christian Vocation in Industry and Marketing* (1926). From this pamphlet we see that Heron was not a revolutionary who happened to be a Christian; he was not even a revolutionary who found the power to be one in his religious faith; his ideas were revolutionary – in the true sense – precisely because they were an attempt to translate the values of the Kingdom into economic practice.

For Heron a religious incentive was not needed in industry merely to make a corrupt system work well – that was the perpetual obsession of religious reformism. It was needed to reconstruct it on quite different principles, issuing in different methods, and therefore enabling it to work well.

Heron invited his audiences and his readers to consider the necessity, value and practicability of organizing industrial enterprises founded explicitly on Christian principles, and of organizing at the same time, as equal departments of Christian practice, the demand and the finance necessary to support and maintain them. He urged, for practical no less than moral reasons, that planning be thought of in terms of goods throughout and not (as was almost exclusively the case) in terms of financial values,

'for goods only collect themselves into inconvenient dumps when marketing consider-
ations are allowed to interfere with our proper use of them.'

Four points stood out in Heron's treatment:

(1) The responsibility of the Church in finding means of deliberately fostering Christian living in industry.

(2) The relation between the Church's doctrine of the living wage and the purchasing power of the community.

(3) The vital interrelation of demand and supply where matters of taste and quality were concerned; and

(4) The many positive assets which truly idealist experiments would enjoy in competition with the soul-less forces of monopoly and 'big business'.

Throughout, Heron protested against the conception that evolution by economic forces would alone lead to a Christian goal.

'Human guidance is needed if human needs are to be met.'

It was only in:

'starting afresh in the humility of minute effort that we can hope to regain the power to guide our working lives. We must re-create in actual practice our philosophy of work and bring it into actual harmony with the highest that we know.'

These were not the pious platitudes of a thinker rather than a doer. Heron's

A works outing in the early days of the T.M. Heron Company, Leeds.

*Keith Ross working on wooden printing blocks watched by Tom Heron
at Cryséde. St Ives, Cornwall.*

thought had been refined by colleagues in industry, by Mirfield Fathers, by his friends in the National Guilds League, the Leeds Arts Club, the Church Socialist League and the League of the Kingdom of God. The doing was in Leeds and Bradford and soon to be in Cornwall and Welwyn Garden City. We turn to triumphs and failures and triumphs again.

Chapter Four

Patron of the ᴄAvant Garde I: Cryséde

CONTINUOUS PARTICIPATION AT THE LEEDS ARTS CLUB and frequent attendance at Orage's soirées at the Cafe Royal in London placed Heron on terms of familiarity with leading avant-garde artists and craftsmen. It was only a short step to his wanting to possess some of their work. As was to be expected of a bachelor running an expanding business, Heron began to enjoy the rôle of patron, a rôle he played with conscious responsibility for the rest of his life whenever his fluctuating fortunes permitted. As a result, the successive homes he and Eulalie set up always struck visitors with their bold choice of highly individual handmade furniture, pottery, fabrics and, of course, paintings, all of which spoke of quality of material and workmanship in a truly modern idiom. The beauty of usefulness and the use of beauty pervaded everything and the whole effect was spiced by the knowledge that many of the artists or craftsmen were friends or relatives. A pot decorated by Roger Fry, lamps, pots and bedroom chairs from Omega Workshops, other pots by Bernard Leach beneath paintings by Jacob Epstein, Jacob Kramer or Bruce Turner set off Simpson's unvarnished oak furniture and rugs and curtains dyed and woven by Ethel Mairet and Heron's sister Kathleen. While still one of Ethel Mairet's first apprentices at Ditchling (1918–20), Kathleen wrote home to her parents:

> 'Mrs Mairet doesn't want to sell the little dress made from my pattern weaving, the one without white. She says it is one of the most beautiful things that has been made in the workshop for months.'

Underlying the impact of contacts with living artists was the lifelong inspiration of William Morris. Though it was the utopian Socialist that had first caught his imagination, it was the artist-craftsman as businessman that was to prove the most fruitful influence, especially as the revival of handicrafts gathered momentum after the 1914–18 war. For the claim to regard Heron as a patron of the avant garde rests much less on his comparatively few purchases from a small purse than on his providing an outlet for creative talent in the commercial world of what may be described loosely as the 'dress trade'. The hand block printing of original designs on silk was to be the hall mark of his business activity, on and off, for nearly thirty years.

The man who occasioned this unexpected change of direction was Alec Walker (1889–1964), son of an established West Riding mill owner from whom Heron had purchased most of the silk for his blouse production in Leeds. The history of their relationship is recalled in Heron's own words:

'My first contact (with Alec Walker) was when I was about sixteen or seventeen and went, as a member of the Undercliffe Hockey Club, to Ravensthorpe to play that club. Both clubs always had two or three county players and the match was always looked forward to. The Ravensthorpe ground was high up on the hillside overlooking the valley, and the changing room was quite a walk from the pitch. It was a cold, wet and windy day and when we got on to the field we found that Ravensthorpe were two men short and the referee would not start the game until they arrived. After what seemed to be an unconscionable time, two players emerged from the mansion house in the valley and marched in state up to the field. They were Alec Walker and his elder brother and we were told that the two mills in the valley belonged to their father, who was 'a hard man' and put each of his sons in charge of a mill. Neither brother made the slightest apology for keeping us all waiting and the rest of their team seemed unwilling to say anything. I remembered this incident five or six years later when I answered an advertisement for a new silk material, "Vigil", which Walker Bros. of Ravensthorpe were wanting to put on the market. I was then running the T. M. Heron Company Ltd. of Buslingthorpe Lane, Leeds, and liked the idea of a British silk which was guaranteed washable and handwoven. I recognized Alec when he came over with his samples and I had no difficulty in persuading him that my "Miona" registered blouses could be a very important customer for "Vigil." We joined forces to advertise "Miona Vigil" blouses and had a great success.'

This insight into the character of Alec Walker is significant in view of the way the two men's careers were to become interwoven – hindsight might suggest the word, 'entangled.' To begin with they had much in common. Both were adventurous young Yorkshiremen, in complementary businesses and with a strong interest in art. Heron said of Walker: 'He had the same ideas about quality that I had.' As manufacturers they re-acted similarly to the post-war slump, wanting to cut their losses, sell off stock cheaply and open up their own retail outlets.

Walker's father was no more flexible than Heron's uncle. While Heron stuck it out in Leeds, Walker escaped to Cornwall, which was already a magnet to artists. In 1918 he married Kathleen Earle, who had been a student at the Stanhope Forbes School of Painting in Newlyn. There they bought a house reputed to have been designed and built by the Adams brothers for themselves. In 1919 Walker bought a short row of fishermen's cottages and converted them into a small factory. The following year he founded Cryséde and began to open shops. While his own production was small, he had to sell bought-in goods as well as his own, including Heron's blouses from Leeds. Silk was sent down from the family business in Yorkshire to Newlyn, where it was bleached, dyed and printed before being made into garments.

Walker was increasingly irked by the tension between his twin ambitions as businessman and artist, for without any formal artistic training, he fancied himself as a modern painter.

Two solutions to his dilemma dramatically improved Walker's fortunes. The first was for Cryséde to print its silks with designs inspired by modern painting. Here he found a niche for himself, providing perfect scope for his own particular artistic talent. The exciting results won widespread recognition, including that of Sir Michael Sadler: 'His work illustrates the new spirit in design, its animation and courage.' The second solution was to free himself from much of the incubus of management. In 1925 he sent an SOS begging Heron to join him. Heron was to manage so that Walker could concentrate on designing. 'If you don't take Cryséde off my back, I will sell it or give it away or close it down.'

The invitation fell into receptive hands. Heron was having a difficult time and beginning to doubt the wisdom of his venture with the Company of English Merchants. He accepted Walker's offer and moved to Cornwall with his family. So Walker weathered his emotional storm.

Phenomenal progress followed Heron's arrival, as with nerve and with verve he began to build on Walker's foundations. Within the first year shops were opened in Bath, Bournemouth, Launceston and Paignton. Cryséde was formed into a limited liability company with greatly increased share capital, of which Walker retained a majority holding. The gross profits for the first sixteen months of £7,020 compared startlingly with the figures for the two preceding years, which averaged £1,092. But the real key to expansion was the move from the cramped premises in Newlyn to the two-acre site in St Ives known as the Island Works. A fourteen-year lease was taken in December 1925. Cryséde moved in the following May and by June about a hundred employees were at work there. In order not to lose its skilled workers in Newlyn, Cryséde bought a Lancia charabanc to fetch them each morning and return them each evening. In between, to help pay for itself, the vehicle provided a daily public service between St Ives and Penzance, and, dovetailed ingeniously into that timetable, it ran afternoon trips from St Ives to Gurnard's Head.

Cryséde prospered and expanded. Already by midsummer 1926 the mail order department, run by Heron's brother-in-law Tal Davies, had 7,000 customers on its books. The quality of its designs and workmanship won a reputation nationally and abroad. In 1928 exhibitions of Cryséde's fabrics, all designed by Walker, were staged in South Africa and Australia. The same year more capital was sought to fund the five extra shops that were to open in 1929, including those in Cheltenham and Cambridge. Half the shareholders were employees.

It is not easy now to realize the impact made on St Ives by the arrival of Cryséde. The sound of the factory hooter briefly drowning the shrieking of gulls was a strange experience at first, but before long people were setting their clocks by it. The town had not known anything like this form of industry, so familiar in Lancashire and the West Riding. There was no tradition of the discipline required for machine work of that sort and Heron had a much harder job training the 'hands' than he had in Leeds, though he found the Cornish girls more perceptive of colour. There were few alternative types of work at that time of rising unemployment, so Cryséde was welcomed with relief, and subsequently with pride, by the wives and daughters of fishermen. They were glad to find a job which was more fulfilling than pickling herrings or taking in summer visitors. Any large, well-organized factory would have impressed St Ives' townsfolk, but the particular nature of the work, involving the creation of beautiful hand-printed silks and lovely dresses, proved unforgettable to many locals. Heron himself was also unforgettable, as Irene Date found after nearly sixty years:

'I was still a schoolgirl living in St Ives and travelling daily by train to the Grammar School at Penzance. I recall vividly the first time I saw this tall, striking, black-bearded figure walking along the seafront at St Ives with two small boys clutching his hands and T. M. H., I am sure, quite oblivious of the quite startling effect he was having on us simple and unsophisticated locals.'

When she heard that Crysède was moving to St Ives, she wrote to ask for a job and thought herself fortunate to be engaged. Emily Woolcock, great-grand-daughter of Alfred Wallis, felt the same. 'If you got in at Crysède, you were "it"!' She too remembered Heron vividly, over forty years after he left Cornwall.

'He was a beautiful man, very upright, very dark beautiful beard, very erect. He always walked with his hands behind his back. He was a marvellous boss but a very strict boss. He would always stop and listen to you. The discipline in that place was marvellous. When Mr Heron used to walk from the office down through there, you could hear a pin drop. We were allowed to sing but not to speak. So you can just imagine what hundreds and hundreds of machines were going like, can't you, and we singing?'

This evocative scene of Crysède comes from Emily's reminiscences taped by Dr Roger Slack in 1974, which are full of detailed information about the Island Works: the boiler that blew up and the generator that 'made their own electric'; the superstitious head cutter who wouldn't cut out anything on a Friday; the parcels being sewn up in cloth instead of being wrapped in paper; the shirt-blouses with thirteen buttonholes down the front and four more on each cuff all sewn by hand. She never forgot the designs: 'Hound and Tree; that tree used to grow right out of the silk. I can see it as plain now as the day it was put on silk.' She probably didn't realize that Crysède's printing of Walker's designs was almost unique in using five, six or even seven different colours. She summed it all up by saying:

'They were wonderful people to work for. It was really a happy place, very very happy, and I remember the day I left, I broke my heart. We were never laid off. Never, never laid off. They always found something for us to do – such as making egg cosies and nightdress cases in winter.'

Patrick Heron also had many vivid memories. As a small boy he was fascinated by the dyeing of silk:

'The dye would be released on to the end of Porthmeor beach, where it would stay in the waves for a whole afternoon.'

Irene Date recalled how the Island Works became a tourist attraction:

'At the Cryséde factory, visitors would be shown the raw woven silk being dyed, washed, finished, etc. and those pieces destined for the printing tables being hand-block printed from hand-carved wooden blocks by skilled and dedicated printers, whose work satisfaction and pride in the finished product were both enormously refreshing and somehow moving. Finally the by now fascinated visitors would queue up for beautifully produced pattern swatches to take away with them, and from them, inevitably, orders for dress lengths etc. would arrive on their return home.'

A notable feature of the memories of Cryséde employees is the rare mention of Alec Walker. This is because of the agreement that Heron was to manage the business while Walker did the designs for it. As the partnership developed, the more Heron did, the happier Walker was to leave him to it. In the forty minutes of her taped reminiscences of Cryséde, Emily Woolcock tells us little about Walker. Irene Date however was more explicit:

'During my three years at Cryséde, I saw Alec Walker but rarely – certainly not more than six times. I seem to remember that one of these visits I missed. I was told that Walker turned up at the factory startling everybody by leading in a horse or a pony he had just bought.'

When the Herons moved to Cornwall, they lodged temporarily at Chywoone Grove above Newlyn and were still there when Joanna was born just before Christmas. Then they were re-united with their furniture and other possessions by renting a small cottage at Lelant, near the sand dunes of the Hayle estuary. They did not feel comfortable there socially. It was a place with a 'posh' golf course for 'toffs,' as Heron said, and neighbours were either remote or snobbish, or both. What about a church? They had not thought much of the parish church, but about eight miles away was the notorious church of St Hilary, under the firecracking leadership of Father Bernard Walke. It did not take the Herons long to find their spiritual home at St Hilary's. The church was unashamedly triumphalist, more ceremoniously Roman than Rome, but with throbbing human warmth and pastoral care. It was a church to raise more than eyebrows. At Joanna's baptism, in accordance with ancient tradition, salt was put on her mouth, a linen cloth over her face and a lighted candle was placed in her tiny hand. The devil was exorcised three times. Having the baby 'done' at St Hilary's was something never to be forgotten. Three years after Joanna it was Giles' turn. Nothing should be read into the fact that for Giles the salt and exorcising aspect of the service was omitted! Not that it was without interest. The name the Herons had chosen was Anthony Giles – the Anthony being Tom's choice as he was fond of Trollope. When Tom, in the service, was asked: 'What name?' he replied: 'Anthony with an 'h' in it.' Father Walke just looked at him and said: 'The saint's name has no 'h' in it', and wrote down Antony. Parish priest and new parishioners were quickly attracted to one another. They were soon having conversations at the vicarage. There was more in common between

Heron and Walke than an interest in talking. Walke was an artist and so was his rather reserved wife. The church was beautifully and imaginatively decorated by Walke. Foxgloves were placed in the grooves of the Gothic pillars. At Christmas four huge ash trees were placed down each side of the chancel with no trimmings except silver tinsel draped round each tree and white candles on the branches. Walke attracted artists from Newlyn who never went to church anywhere else. 'Come to St Hilary's and I will show you how to use your gifts to the glory of God.' Eight of them painted small frescoes round the chancel. There were plays in church and good music and poetry. Above all there was worship. Walke, albeit something of a benevolent despot – and not always benevolent, knew how to help people worship. One of the most moving scenes in the year was at the end of the Midnight Mass at Christmas, when the whole of the packed congregation knelt round the crib. Events such as that affected Heron's senses and emotions as well as his mind. He never forgot it.

The demands of the business and the needs of the growing family did not leave the Herons with much time for social life apart from St Hilary's, but they made friends easily, often for life. One such was the potter, Bernard Leach. Eulalie's letters often refer to the Leaches, country dancing on their lawn, helping with teas on open day at the pottery, and so on. They corresponded once the Herons lived in Hertfordshire. In 1930 Bernard wrote to Eulalie about closing the gap between factory and workshop:

'You say I'm an individual potter for individuals. Tom an industrialist for the populace. I say that I want to provide decent pots for ordinary folk and I believe he can do the same with textiles, although he works with a small factory and I with a large studio.'

Forty years on Leach and Heron were exchanging poems they had written and welcoming comments. By then their interest centred on religious philosophy and comparing old age. In 1974 Leach wrote through an amanuensis:

'Yes, I have come to the end of reading, writing, drawing and all visual arts, but there is no end as long as life itself continues, that is, for ever.'
'As I see it, the western world has lost both faith and humility and cannot meet the other half until those conditions are regained. In fact the western world must come back to its knees.'

Other friends were the Arnold-Forsters. Will was the Labour candidate for whom Heron canvassed in the 1929 General Election. They lived at Eagle's Nest, perched above the cliffs near Zennor, where Will had created a fabulous garden.

They let the house to the Herons for the five winter months 1927–8, hoping it might abate Patrick's asthma. A letter from Eulalie shortly before leaving Cornwall recorded:

'Mrs A-Forster called on me on Saturday afternoon – very friendly and so sorry we're going. She brought me in a box a most wonderfully beautiful Eastern Passion flower, rich and lovely beyond words. I floated it in a small blue bowl on water.'

By 1929 the business was a runaway success but tragedy was already gathering in the wings. Alec Walker's personal life was complicated. He had fallen deeply in love with a colonel's daughter. The colonel was a country gentleman whose style of life embraced riding and hunting. Walker wanted this life-style for himself and pursued both it and the daughter. He wanted to divorce his wife. After some two years of dalliance, the daughter refused him. Pursuing county life or cloistered in his Newlyn studio, Walker had hardly been seen in the Island Works for sixteen months. People remembered the cottage industry at Newlyn and compared it with the flourishing business they saw Heron managing in St Ives. Walker became jealous. The success of his brainchild was being attributed to Heron. The jealousy was exacerbated by the knowledge that Heron's friends, many of whom visited him in St Ives, included artists, sculptors and critics of national reputation. Walker was becoming aware of his own limitations as a painter. It did not help him to see the remarkable early artistic talent of Heron's son Patrick being fostered with the imaginative parental understanding he himself had had to struggle without.

With the collapse of Walker's personal life, he suddenly wanted Cryséde back and all for himself. He became bitter, arrogant and twisted. He said to Heron: 'I am responsible to God alone for this business. *You* are responsible to *me*.'

Walker's determination to resume the helm of management at Cryséde was to lead to the dismissal of Heron and much of the talented team he had assembled. Cryséde never recovered from these amputations.

Heron was accused of interfering with Walker's love affair. That was true in so far as Heron made an effort to keep the Walkers together, even lending them his house in St Ives for a long, and as it turned out final, talk together. Heron was also accused of trying to get Walker to church. That too was partially true for Heron was not above proselytizing and felt that the parish and parish priest of St Hilary's might help to give Walker the stability he needed.

It was June 1929 and Heron and Walker met to see if they could come to an arrangement, if not an agreement, as to their business future. They paced to and fro along the jetty. Eulalie was sitting on the nearby hillside. She describes the conclusion with saddening succinctness:

'At last Tom came up to me and said, "It's no good; we shall have to go. I can't keep my self-respect and work under the conditions Alec proposes." So he was given the sack and six months' salary and we left.'

The rise and fall of Cryséde reads like a Greek tragedy. It is a story of brilliant promise undermined by a flaw in the personality of its founder that grew like a cancer to destroy the firm and its central characters, including Walker himself. His had been the germinal inspiration and his designing talent its greatest original asset. Alas, his too was the instability, the inner conflict of ambitions and, finally the destructive jealousy. He blew out his own glittering candle.

Chapter Five

Patron of the Avant Garde II: The Creation of Cresta

CRYSÉDE WAS OVER FOR HERON. It had been an enterprise inspired by artistic flair and social purpose. Expanding rapidly under his charismatic management, it had gathered momentum like a rocket and like a rocket it created dazzling beauty which lingered in the eye long after the sparks had gone out and the sky returned to a dark void. For a while that darkness must have seemed impenetrable to the Herons. As with most traumatic experiences, there was great need and scope for soul-searching but the pressing practical problems of finding a new job and a new home would not wait for calm reflection.

There followed, through the summer of 1929, a period of extreme anxiety and effort for both of them, a period of trial reminiscent of fairy tales in which the metal of heroes and heroines is put to the test. Like Dick Whittington, Tom set off for London to seek his fortune with little more than his experience, his idealism and his courage. For almost seven weeks Eulalie waited at St Ives with the four children. She had to practice urgent economy, bread and jam without butter, water instead of lemonade. She stopped using the phone; she looked for lodgers; she tried to sell the house; she washed and mended the clothes Tom sent each week from London; she kept him in touch with the worsening situation at Cryséde. Perhaps the process of self-examination for both of them was all the more effective because they faced it three hundred miles apart, communicating only by post. Enough of that correspondence remains to show the depth of their shock and the strength of their determination to understand the causes of failure and to learn from them. Since this crisis and its resolution epitomize the essential character of Heron's whole business career and of his marriage too, it is worth while quoting at length from one of Eulalie's remarkable letters:

'You know darling there are two strains in you. There's the part of you that wants to 'make good' in business in the ordinary way – as Ben Dawson and Hitchin and Uncle Jim have done. You know that you have the ability and could do as well as they – and you know how well you could use the money if you made it. You think of what you could do for the boys and what a lovely home we could have. Then there's the other side of you, with your vision of the Kingdom of God in industry – and you want to do something to establish that in the world. And up to now you have fallen between two stools. You want the reward that goes to the Ben Dawsons – together with the satisfaction of working for your ideal, and find yourself at the moment left without either.

You weren't worldly-wise enough to make sure of your own interests in Crysède – and you also find that you haven't cared supremely about the other thing because there has been a mixture of self-glorification in it.'

Before receiving this analysis, Tom had already come to some of the same conclusions:

'What I am beginning to feel now,' he wrote from London, 'is that in business I have been trying to be not as other men were but a paragon of righteousness, shining in a world of sin. Well, that's hit on the head now. And dear, it's been the same in my marriage. I was getting too big to be an ordinary husband and father.'

Understandably his letters were fewer and shorter than hers. He had left Cornwall with various possible schemes in mind, the irreducible core of which was the establishment of a new business manufacturing and selling quality silk. He was living out of a suitcase, away from home, without the aid of office or secretary. His days were spent in a constant whirl of activity as he sought one person after another he thought could help. At nights his brain teemed with ideas, assimilating responses, weaving them into his plans and deciding on the morrow's round of contacts. The pressure of creative work revived his energy and self-confidence. His powers of persuasion blossomed. At each promise of support, new possibilities opened up demanding immediate attention, so that he was repeatedly postponing his return to St Ives, even for the shortest and most desperately-needed respite. He did not allow himself that luxury until he felt assured of the future as to both business and home.

Heron's achievement in those weeks of concentrated activity was a 'tour de force.' Starting from scratch, he had obtained promises of sufficient funding to establish a new business manufacturing quality dresses of silk made to its own specification by the oldest silk mill in the country, to be sold in its own chain of shops. He had arranged for Price Waterhouse to proceed with the legal formalities of creating the company and had opened negotiations for premises for its headquarters in Welwyn Garden City. He had gone on to secure the further backing of the established reputable family business of the Heathcote-Amory's at Tiverton, who were to enjoy a majority shareholding. He was also well on the way with the process of putting together a board of directors and a team of senior staff, the latter including the cream of the talent he had assembled at St Ives. In short he had laid the foundations of Cresta Silks Limited, one of the notable British textile firms of the twentieth century. Meanwhile the Crysède board of directors had removed Walker himself – he was certified unfit for business – and implored Heron to return. It was too late. At the end of July Eulalie had written: 'I am longing to begin the new life.' She didn't have to wait much longer. By September the whole family was installed in Welwyn Garden City and the new adventure had begun.

However, it was not to be plain sailing. Heron was navigating in dangerous waters, all the more so after the Wall Street crash of November 1929. When it was busy coping with all the obvious difficulties of the ensuing economic depression, the newly-launched Cresta was nearly wrecked by the removal of the two main planks of Heron's financial support. James Barlow (Eulalie's wealthy Uncle Jim), who was Chairman of the Board of Directors, lost most of his fortune and had to pull out. Worse was to follow. The deteriorating conditions of trade strained the partnership between Heron and Heathcotes. Their different reactions to danger were incompatible. Heathcotes' instinct was to play safe and revert to conventional tactics: Heron's was to trust in the organic development of his own original vision. Heathcotes lacked instinctive appreciation of avant-garde design and of the potential of Welwyn Garden City. In order to sell more, or even all, of their own production through Cresta, they wanted rapid expansion and proposed to acquire an existing chain of shops and possibly an existing, larger factory, in Leeds, say, or the East End of London. Heron could not agree to what he saw as the destruction of the essential character of his creation. Heathcotes informed Heron they wished to replace him as Managing Director with a member of their own firm, a certain Mr Smith. They would buy Heron out. Heron asked if they would give him three weeks to raise money to buy them out instead. They agreed.

Once again Heron had his back to the wall. On this occasion time was not on his side for he was up against a deadline and it was, if anything, a more difficult moment in 1932 to inspire confidence and raise money than it had been three years earlier. On the other hand, he had something to show. To the discerning, the quality of Cresta was more than mere speculation and in Welwyn Garden City there were those who appreciated what Cresta could bring to the local community, notably Dick Reiss, Leonard Gray and John Eccles, all key figures in the town's development.

As the deadline approached, Heron was still over £1500 short of the goal. 'It's all up,' he said to Eulalie, 'I haven't been able to make it.' As they sat and faced this new disaster, into their home walked Dick and Celia Reiss. 'How is it doing?'

When Tom explained the gravity of the situation, Dick said 'Oh! didn't you understand that we were putting up that amount?' The day was saved, Heathcotes withdrew, perhaps with relief, and Heron was left in control assisted by a Board of Directors so united in purpose and mutual respect that he was proud to assert in later years that they never voted as a way of reaching decisions but 'talked things through' to agreement. Leonard Gray took over as Chairman in May 1933 and presided in that capacity for over twenty years.

The creation and development of Cresta between 1929 and 1939 marked the pinnacle of Heron's achievement in business. Long after it ceased to exist it was remembered vividly by a great and varied company of admirers; indeed its name still evokes interest and admiration as the twenty-first century opens. It is time to consider in what way it was so remarkable.

To understand the nature of Cresta Silks, one must realize that it was the creation of Heron's maturity, the fruit of all his previous experience and the incarnation of his personal philosophy of work, which was in turn the central theme of his whole adult life. He had long recognized that different basic types of human nature had to work in different patterns, different rhythms, if they were to find personal fulfilment: the artist, the teacher, the businessman, the priest – all of whom he had been able to observe among his close relations – and many more. In Cresta he was deliberately blending the distinct patterns of work needed by everyone involved from the machinist to the fashion stylist, the shop-assistant to the Board Director, the typist to the boiler-man. Into this matrix each specialized activity had to be fitted harmoniously; nobody's work should exclude her (or him) from sharing a common purpose, a common pride; human relationships were to be more akin to those of a family than those dictated primarily by market forces. Of course the firm must pay its way, handsomely if possible, but pay should be the reward, not the prime purpose, of work.

This integration or integrity – Heron would have regarded them as inseparable – can be seen strikingly in the close relation between two of the basic principles on which Cresta was founded. One was the pursuit of quality in everything; the other was the placing of the creative artist at the centre of the whole plan. Almost the first step Heron had taken in planning Cresta was to secure his supply of raw material. The silk was especially woven on old looms at Arnold Wright's Silk Mill at Sherborne, Dorset, of silks whose yarns had not been submitted to the greater strain imposed by the speedier, modern equipment. Not content with that, all Cresta's silks were submitted to the Lux Washing Tests at Lever Brothers' Laboratories, as an impressed reporter for the *Welwyn Times* explained in January 1930:

> 'Any silk not passing these searching tests is returned to the dyer or weaver and does not pass until the manufacturer is satisfied that as far as is humanly possible, perfection has been reached.'

People coming across Cresta for the first time could see – literally – that everything about it reflected the quality of visual excitement and purpose. Those who paused long enough would notice the harmony between the excellence of the silk, the designs printed upon it, the style of the dresses it was made into, the external and internal architecture of shops and workrooms and their accessories, down to the logo on boxes and notepaper. Some felt that the pervasive harmony extended to the mood and behaviour of those who worked there.

It is not surprising therefore that among the first-rate modern artists whom Heron employed from the very beginning at Cresta were those who shared more than aesthetic convictions. Straight away, before 1929 was out, he had commissioned designs from Paul Nash, whom he had met long ago in Leeds and whose paintings he had enjoyed over many years since. Nash was to be President of the Society of Industrial Artists and held views close to those of Herbert Read – Heron's Leeds days again! – who, as so often, championed the cause of the artist. On the question of the relationship between art and industrial design Read wrote:

> 'Designers should not be required merely to produce a number of sketches on paper which will be left to the mercy of factory management and salesmen to adapt to the

Two of Cresta's early hand-printed designs. Above: 'Cherry Orchard', dress fabric, Paul Nash, c.1931. Below: 'Melon', silk square, Patrick Heron, 1934.

imaginary demands of the public: the artist must design in the actual materials of the factory and in the full steam of the process of production.'

Though this description did not exactly fit the way Cresta designs were produced, Read would have approved of the close co-operation and mutual respect between Heron and the artists he employed. It was always a personal as well as a professional relationship. The artists appreciated the meticulous care insisted on in achieving exact colour and detail to satisfy both the designer and Heron himself, even if, as in the case of Nash, this could drag out the work for an extra six months. Heron never advertised for designers. They were artists whose work he liked. Sometimes it was he who persuaded them to design in the first place, as with his Leeds friend Bruce Turner, and of course with his own son Patrick, whose first design – the silk square 'Melon' – was done when he was only fourteen. The most prolific Cresta designer up to the outbreak of war was Cedric Morris, whom Heron had met in Newlyn. Morris had visited the Cryséde factory at St Ives to see what was going on and expressed a desire to try his hand at designing textiles. Heron remembered this when starting up Cresta. 'I thought his love of flowers and his painting showed that he was a designer.' There was a problem with the size of the flowers, which Heron solved characteristically.

'I made certain that the dress designer knew the limitations of textile designing and that the textile designer knew what the dress designer had to have.'

These were the artists who worked most regularly for Cresta but there were others engaged from time to time, such as John Armstrong, whose design was used for a prestigious commission as the *Welwyn Times* proudly reported on its front page on January 28th 1932:

'The new Stratford-on-Avon theatre, now nearing completion, is architecturally extremely interesting and will probably be the most talked of building of the year. It is decidedly a feather in the cap of Cresta Silks Ltd that they should have secured the order for the theatre curtains.'

If the quality of Cresta Silks' printed designs was consistently outstanding, the story of its architecture was even more remarkable, revealing Heron's flair for patronage in a new dimension. Wells Coates' Cresta shops were a brilliant innovation on the English scene. It is now possible to regard him as the first talent to mature among English architects representative of the Modern Movement and as one of its central figures. It is clear that Wells Coates' career as an architect and his belated recognition stem directly from Heron's daring commission to design all the early Cresta shops and its first factory. Once again, Heron showed his gift for spotting rare talent and knowing how to use it, and once again it depended on personal chemistry. It was daring indeed to stake so much of the new firm's future on the work of a man who had had no formal architectural training of any sort. Wells Coates' background was hardly promising. Born in Japan of Canadian parents –

the one a professor of theology and the other a missionary – he had a first degree in engineering and a Ph.D. for work on diesel engine gasses. He had been an RAF pilot during the war and more recently a *Daily Express* journalist. Yet Heron recognized Wells Coates' unusual latent talent and saw that it was searching for an outlet corresponding closely with his own, equally unusual requirements. Heron wanted shops that would attract the discerning customers who would buy his dresses, and workrooms that would assist those engaged in designing and making them. The aura of architecture and dresses had to be complementary. Wells Coates, believing in the importance of the functional aspect of architecture, was ready to provide that link. In keeping with the inherent obsession of artists with what is new, Wells Coates was drawn towards the use of the latest materials technology provided, which at that time included plate glass, plywood and metal. These, being comparatively cheap, were not necessarily expected to last for ever. Heron had limited capital to spare on architecture – or anything else! – and in any case was averse to extravagant, showy use of expensive materials. Wells Coates' contemporary and relatively temporary and inexpensive architecture fitted well with Heron's way of affording a foothold for Cresta in the most prestigious shopping areas. He achieved this by taking short-term leases where long ones would have been pro-hibitively expensive. As a result, Wells Coates' earlier commissions, apart from the first factory at Welwyn, included his Cresta shops in Brompton Road, Bond Street, Bournemouth and Brighton. Wells Coates' predilection for plate glass accorded perfectly with Heron's determination to let in as much daylight as possible to improve working conditions and to enable customers and workers alike to judge the true colours of Cresta's wares.

Another of Heron's principles, that every item of furnishing should be integrated into the over-all scheme of design, suited Wells Coates down to the ground. Uninhibited by any narrow conception of what was or was not the traditional architect's rôle, he was eager to tackle a wide range of technical problems, so everything bore the stamp of his hand: the radiators, cushion-stools, tubular-steel lamp standards, sliding plate-glass wardrobe doors, and, of course, his famous 'D' door handles.

The two men appreciated each other's priorities. Their collaboration proved of mutual benefit. Cresta materials and dresses in the windows set off Wells Coates' architecture to perfection and the clientèle the goods attracted began to enhance his reputation. Conversely, the clean lines and economy of the architecture caught the attention of suitable potential customers and reinforced the Cresta image of stylish, quality clothes at moderate prices.

The attention paid to Wells Coates' shops on purely architectural grounds provided Cresta with valuable free advertisement, as professional journals carried critiques of his work. One journalist's verdict on the Brighton shop concluded:

'This shop has considerable interest and beauty. The economy yet boldness of its forms have an abiding appeal and for my part please me in every way.'

Cresta's First shop:
Brompton Road, SW3, designed by Wells Coates 1929.

Two further quotations may illustrate how much there was in common between the attitudes of architect and client. In 1932 Wells Coates wrote:

'As architects of the human and material scenes of the new order, we are not so much concerned with formal problems of styles as with an architectural solution of the social and economic problems of today.'

An article in the *Welwyn Times* in 1933 recognised that Cresta had a wider purpose than most manufacturing concerns:

'The firm has a philosophy of clothes. It believes not only that clothes express personality but that they actually affect the future of civilization.'

Wells Coates' striking work did not of course please everybody all the time. Miss Crump, Cresta's chief stylist for many years, found it insufficiently feminine and apparently Heron appreciated this. At the first Brompton Road shop, Wells Coates' famous cubist, three-dimensional letters C.R.E.S.T.A. (horizontal) and S.I.L.K.S. (smaller, vertical, facing sideways) were redesigned in a more elegant, curvilinear style by McKnight Kauffer. It was another inspired choice of artist in the opening months of Cresta's development which led to McKnight Kauffer's designing the firm's eye-catching stationery and cardboard boxes. Both carried the insignia he invented, a device which epitomized the style Heron was pursuing. McKnight Kauffer also designed very effective advertisements for Cresta. He became famous subsequently for his London Transport posters and has been described as the outstanding graphic designer in Britain at that time.

Brutalizing ugliness was only one of the aspects of working conditions in the textile industry of the West Riding that had first roused the young Heron to wrath, and which it was a central purpose of his career in business to reform. Those working for Cresta were never likely to be starved of visual beauty, but that alone would not account for the degree of their job satisfaction or their loyalty to the firm and to Heron personally. Each time he moved, some of his employees chose to follow him, from Leeds to St Ives, from St Ives to Welwyn Garden City. Maud Watt stayed with him all the way. The speed with which the new Cresta got into its stride – the factory/headquarters/shop in Welwyn, two more shops in London and one each in Bournemouth and Brighton, all opened in the first fifteen months – that speed owed a great deal to the people Heron brought with him from Cryséde, especially his brother-in-law Tal Davies, who was a Director from the start, the memorably soignée and gifted dress-designer Honey Bowen, and Irene Date, whose entire working life, after three years at Cryséde, was spent at Cresta.

The tradition of personal relations was established while it was still a case of 'small is beautiful', and though Cresta grew too large for Heron to be sure he knew every individual employee, they all felt that they knew him. There was no place for trade unions in Cresta. Miss Crump remembered the occasion when the unions wanted to send someone down to talk to the girls and she and Heron had to go out for lunch. 'Thank God,' the girls said, 'We're not going to pay them! Why

McKnight Kauffer's lettering for Cresta.
above: Company Notepaper
below: Cresta Shop, Bond Street 1933.

should we? We're happy as we are!' Peggy Barlow, who was a Director for fourteen of her thirty-four years at Cresta, stressed Heron's belief in the value of a happy and contented staff:

'He was always a paternal figure to the staff.' ... 'Cresta was always a very personal business. He was ready at any time to listen to any member of staff who was in trouble or difficulty and would go to great lengths to help and advise. Cresta developed into a close-knit family.'

In those years of economic depression Heron regarded his power of employment as a social responsibility. He offered jobs to people not only because of their ability but also because of their need. Sentiment counted as well as business, as Cresta found work for unemployed people from distressed areas like Jarrow, for refugees from Hitler's Germany, or for those suffering a broken marriage. Possibly there were some passengers aboard at times but often unforeseen competence emerged.

Heron's way of achieving a contented and industrious work force made little use of conventional sticks and carrots. He preferred to rely on imaginative organization. In spite of being radical in a great many ways, he was never tempted to embark on industrial democracy in determining policy, though a notable element of democracy was enjoyed socially. There was, for instance, no preferential treatment or segregation by rank in the canteen or in the provision of toilets. He rejected piece-work because it tended towards inferior workmanship. Another practice Cresta avoided was the more extreme application of the division of labour which would have left a girl repeating an operation monotonously, gaining skill and speed in cuffs or button-holing but without any pride in the whole garment. At Cresta girls were taught hand-sewing before advancing to machine-work; then they were moved round, gaining proficiency in each process in turn, until they had learned every task and could make a complete dress, when they even did their own pressing. One such girl, Joan Goodman, left school at fourteen in 1935. She was still working at Cresta as a designer in 1975, when the local paper carried an article in celebration of her forty years' service. Her mother, sister and daughters all worked for Cresta too. She particularly cherished memories of 'a very happy working atmosphere, of the firm's outings on the River Thames in summer and family-like Christmas parties.' Heron often showed an interest in the families of his employees, as they did in his, and letters they wrote show that to them he was not just the 'Boss' but something of a friend, too. Norman Vibert wrote from St Ives some time after Heron had left:

'You have always been interested in my family so you will like to know that we have another increase; that makes eight of us now.'

In 1956 Heron received a letter from Leeds, over thirty years after he had left:

'I am Eleanor Wood, late Walker, who I use to work for you at Buslingthorpe Lane I work for you for 12 years up to you close down and if you had been in Leeds now I'll still work for you.'

Letters written to Joanna's daughter Rosalind in 1983 included one from Mrs Hayman, who worked at Cresta for thirty-five years. 'If at any time you could write and let me know how all the family are – I should love that. Those years were very happy ones for me.' And Beatrice, née Stebbings, who joined the firm in 1933 and continued with it until 1977 wrote: 'I saw your mother grow up. I made suits for Mrs Heron, usually from hand-woven cloth, woven by Miss Kathleen Heron.'

The commercial success of the company depended on more than the quality of design and crafting by a contented staff. Irene Date, who was well placed to see the business perspective, praised Heron for 'an astute awareness of a need for the kind of merchandise and service he envisaged Cresta could provide.' Alan Powers, historian of modern block-printed textiles, is more specific. 'Much of Cresta's success lay in identifying a clientèle between couture and mass-market appropriate for the hard times of the 1930's.' Usually the combination of personal service and the highest quality of materials and design was only within the reach of the very well off. Cresta's rare achievement was to offer that combination at more moderate prices and it was able to do this because it controlled every stage of production from the loom to the shop counter, cutting out all middlemen. The niche Heron identified for Cresta was not à la mode. Instead of striving for what is in fashion tomorrow, he aimed for enduring styles that enhance the form in every period. The word used so often to describe Cresta styles was 'classic.' Since it is not every woman that can walk into off-the-rail, ready-made dresses, however good those dresses may be, Cresta's niche extended to the development of a very skilled special order department. Each shop had its own workroom and kept its customers' measurements, so it could order whole dresses, not just carry out skilled alterations.

A very belated search for evidence of customers' opinions of Cresta was made in 1982, well after the firm ceased to exist. The number of responses, besides the praise and fond memories they contained, was confirmation of its reputation and achievement. Besides showing how dearly Cresta clothes were cherished, they portray the women for whom Heron had been catering so thoughtfully. One lady wrote simply 'in gratitude for endless satisfaction.' Another took the trouble to sketch two of her war-time dresses under the title: 'Cresta. Lovely Happy Clothes.' Another actually sent a red silk coat her mother used to wear at Ascot. 'My mother always shopped at Cresta. So did I.'

The public at large was aware that besides being a commercial business, Cresta embodied some sort of idealism. Most did not realize, however, just how idealistic Heron's motivation was. One who did was Joseph Thorpe, drama critic of *Punch*, another of those colourful characters of whom Heron's life was so full. Thorpe 'fell' for Welwyn Garden City, met Heron, was captivated by Cresta and became a Director for a few years. He wrote promotional items including a highly innovative six-page inset in *The Countryman* which appeared in 1934. The choice of journal was in itself evidence of Cresta's awareness of its unique clientèle. In what he ambitiously entitled *Cresta Quarterly*, Thorpe wrote of his initiative:

'It is not just a business device. It is to concern itself (in its modest way) with a philosophy of dress and a philosophy of work; with a possible future nexus between consumer and producer other than that of buyer and seller; and it may have some bearing on those changes in the structure of industry which are in the minds of the thoughtful at the present time.'

Heron used different images to explain his idealism -

'"Seek ye first the Kingdom of Heaven" etc. has always been one of the sayings that has influenced me. I keep testing my new scheme (Cresta) by this and however clever I may be at wangling, I don't find any necessary here. "The Kingdom of Heaven is within you" becomes clearer to me! The how I conduct my business and the how I guard my thoughts seems much more important than the form my business takes.'

Regardless of how little or how much its philosophy was understood, Cresta throve. It became clear that a bigger factory was needed to supply the additional shops being planned and Heron set to work with such characteristic flair and energy that in 1938 the whole business was able to move into spacious new premises in Howardsgate. Though its policy of combining factory, offices and shop on a single site contributed to efficient operation and cohesion, Cresta was handicapped at Broadwater Road with regard to its shop, since Broadwater Road was in the heart of the industrial zone of the town, remote from most customers' homes and most other shops. Securing the site in Howardsgate was something of a coup for Heron, who converted the combination of function from a disadvantage to an asset. Normally the town's strict planning regulation did not allow factories to the west of the railway, but an exception was made of Cresta because its factory lay hidden behind its shop, with which, Heron argued, it needed to be in constant close touch. Many regarded the new Cresta shop as enjoying the best site in the town, fronting the main boulevard and immediately adjacent to the railway station, so that West End shoppers and daily commuters alike were subject to the lure of those wonderful silks. Furthermore, the Cresta site included vacant land to the rear, so that even this new, larger building could be more than doubled in future. The only drawback from Heron's point of view was that Welwyn Garden City Company's planning policy insisted on a common, neo-Georgian, style for the fronts of all the buildings on Howardsgate, so he was denied the opportunity to patronize a truly modern architect. There was, of course, scope for a few innovations such as double-glazing, sandwiching burglar-alarm wiring which was connected directly to the police station. The best thing about the new building was its position and its space. It engendered a spirit of optimism.

Chapter Six

War and the Board of Trade

THE YEAR 1939 FOUND TOM HERON IN THE PRIME OF LIFE. His third of a century of business experience had been a hard schooling, from which he was emerging with flying colours. Cresta had carved itself a small but unique niche in the world of fashion; its reputation was already established and fields of expansion and further artistic adventure were opening up before it.

The war which broke in on the lives of individuals and institutions alike in September 1939 destined many never to see the light of peace again. No knowledgeable punter would have laid serious money on the survival of Cresta, a firm dealing almost exclusively in top quality silks and workmanship, designed by avant-garde artists, hand-printed by craftsmen for a clientèle of the discerning and better off. Surely there was no place for luxury in a 'total' war? For a rare moment Heron assumed the worst and gave his employees notice. Then he regained his nerve and rescinded it, but a few, alas, had gone. Most were only too glad to stay.

In the event, both Heron and Cresta were to survive the war but it was never rosy dawn again. As the destruction of war was unleashed and a series of necessarily harsh measures forged Britain's war economy, abject pessimism would have been amply justified. All silk on order was requisitioned by the Government for parachutes; home market sales of textile goods were progressively and severely restricted; Cresta's splendid new headquarters, combining offices, factory and shop, were commandeered and workers were conscripted for the forces or directed to war-work. Clothing prices rose sharply as fuller employment and higher wages produced inflationary pressure offset by increases in existing taxation – income tax up to 10/- and the imposition of new forms of tax such as purchase tax.

Anyone less resilient and with less experience of trading in adverse circumstances would have gone under or thrown in the sponge, but Heron fought on, living from hand to mouth, redirecting his business to the single aim of survival, to keep enough of the firm intact to act as a springboard for revival whenever peace might return.

With radical courage, he decided to deal in wool instead of silk. He went up to Bradford and bought 'a tremendous lot of woollen dress goods', which the slump in trade had left available. This purchase enabled Cresta to remain in business long after fresh supplies had begun to dry up. Displaying similarly bold strategic initiative, he opened a shop in Bristol (in 1940!) as an insurance against Cresta's vulnerability in having headquarters near London. (Ironically it was the Bristol shop that was badly damaged by bombs while Welwyn escaped!)

He made do with all sorts of improvized jobs, such as the provision and fitting of blackout curtains, and moved all his operations into a portion of Welwyn Stores, the huge departmental stores only recently opened by the Welwyn Garden City Company. He found himself alternative employment for four years and placed the day-to-day management in the capable hands of Irene Date, restricting his own essential supervision and guidance to Saturday mornings and free time.

While Heron had his plate full of Cresta problems, he nevertheless found his shrinking business allowed him time to ponder on the plethora of red-tape and the gaping insecurity of all businesses. What he saw was the painfully slow evolution by trial and error of a policy for clothing the nation in wartime. Hesitation and inconsistency betrayed the lack of inside experience and understanding of textile and clothing manufacture on the part of the politicians and officials struggling with the task. They were also hindered by the subordination of their interests to other Ministries which carried more clout. Churchill himself obstructed the overdue introduction of clothes rationing when eventually the Board of Trade was trying to implement it in the spring of 1941.

Heron could not survey the scene with alarm and do nothing about it. We find him writing articles and letters in the *New English Weekly* and letters to *The Times* on cartels, education, war aims, peace aims, and, of course, clothing. He was incensed at the wasteful and nonsensical use of wool and said so in a letter to *The Times* and in the long and forceful memorandum he sent to the Government. That memorandum, the product of purely personal initiative on his part, proved a turning point in Heron's career and led to his important contribution to clothing the nation in war-time It could not have reached the Board of Trade at a more opportune moment.

It had been recognized on the eve of the war that standardization would be the only way of ensuring supplies of necessities at reasonable prices, once resources of manpower and materials were severely limited, but standardization of so fragmentary an industry as that of clothing was an intractable problem. Understandably, the Conservative-led Coalition Government shrank from the Socialist logic of managing the industry itself. When at last the War Cabinet approved a scheme in March 1940, there was little confidence the scheme would work and it was buried for a year while the argument shifted to the complementary question of rationing. Heron's Memorandum set out the principles that were to break the deadlock and form the basis of what became known as the Utility Clothing Scheme, the central stategy by which the Government achieved both quantity and quality of production of civilian clothing, and also its more satisfactory distribution.

To understand how it was that the managing director of a very small private firm was in a position to offer such valuable advice to the Board of Trade, one must consider both the state of the industry and the experience of the man.

The British clothing industry had developed haphazard like Topsy. It had little unifying principle beyond the common goal of each of thousands of private initiatives to exploit a perceived need and reap the reward of profit within the freedom of the market economy. Individual firms may have been efficient, but the structure of the industry was chaotic. Consequently, when war-time Departments used their unparalleled emergency powers to enforce policies which substituted national for private needs, they were often found unworkable or had unfortunate side effects. For example, the regulation limiting firms to a percentage of their previous production ignored the factor of where stocks happened to be and created distribution problems, and since quotas were measured per yard or per garment, manufacturers were led to concentrate on making their most expensive materials or garments instead of their cheaper ones. Even measures comparatively simple in principle foundered on the complexity of local practice, as in the case of the Government's 'concentration' policy, whereby some of the firms who could no longer make full use of their plant and labour released them for essential war work, while production was 'concentrated' in the remainder. However, application of this policy to clothing was said to be 'administratively difficult and politically untouchable' because the industry was made up of so many small and diverse firms.

When the Board of Trade set out to regulate retail trade it had no idea how many retail shops there were, because basic statistical evidence was often lacking; so, sometimes, was accepted common terminology – Heron later had to travel to Glasgow to establish when a garment was a kilt!

Anyone sharing his belief in vocation would be excused for seeing Heron's previous career as a preparation to move on to the national stage. At a time when the processes converting raw materials into the clothes on people's backs were generally compartmentalized, he had acquired an intimate working knowledge of many and an easy familiarity with the rest. After growing up among the woollen mills of Bradford and serving his time as an agent in cloth, he had created businesses in the making-up trade, unusually combining production with retail through his own shops. His experience extended through wool, cotton, linen and silk, from printing techniques to fashion styling, from Yorkshire and Cornwall to London. He had continued active business throughout the 1914–1918 war and had ridden the troughs and peaks of peacetime slumps and boom.

Equally at home in the boardroom and on the factory floor, used to rubbing shoulders with craftsmen and financiers, he respected the needs of employees, customers and tax-collectors alike. Perhaps the legacy of his earlier involvement with Fabianism and Guild Socialism helped to open his mind to the possibilities of an industry that permitted private enterprise to continue operating under strong central control. His virtue was to see both the wood and the trees.

A close comparison of Heron's Memorandum of the first week in April 1941 with the Utility Clothing Scheme as it was to develop, reveals the great extent to which that scheme bore the stamp of his personal business philosophy and experience. As usual his pragmatism and idealism were inseparable.

'If the right scheme is now adopted, when wartime restrictions are abolished the industry will find itself pointing its efforts in the right direction. If cutting down is required, let it be as far as possible a pruning which has future growth in view. The kind of co-operation required in an industry is that which grows naturally from an understanding of the real nature of that industry and of the function which individuals and groups in it can best perform. Whether only the minimum of clothing has to be issued, or whether plenty can be released does not affect what might be called the Natural Law for the Ladies' Clothing Trade.'

Quality and style were the key to Heron's proposals and it was quality of design and material that were to be the key to the renowned success of Utility Clothing.

'In theory, styling should always be based on the functional. In wartime it is absolutely essential that it should be. The number of people who want to create styles and are capable of doing so to the satisfaction of the buying public is fairly limited. Most clothing concerns only want to keep going. They buy styles (or steal them) and adapt them to their requirements. Often when copying a style, either from lack of knowledge or from a desire for excessive cheapness, they lose its point both from the aesthetic and from the practical point of view. It is suggested that under the new scheme the styles and the patterns for them should be given to the various producers, or at any rate sold to them at fixed charge.'

Heron realized that the successful standardization of clothing depended upon replacing the existing mass of largely inferior styles by the best designs possible. He also saw that under the constraints of wartime austerity, only the best designers in the country could meet the needs of the aesthetic function of dress:

'In wartime, as in peacetime, it is important that women in all walks of life should feel comfortable in their clothes and should know that they are suitably dressed for whatever work they have to do. If there is to be a scarcity of clothes, it is all the more reason why we should see that the industry is organized to produce the right ones. Most of the thousands of styles now produced are not really wanted by anyone. They have been produced for a selling technique which the war is abolishing. Apart from uniforms and overalls, the wartime dress requirements of women can best be met by the production of a few styles only, provided these have been carefully thought out.'

After outlining the sort of committee structure for approving the styles to be promoted by the scheme, Heron drew on his practical experience yet again in emphasizing the important relationship between style and size:

'Each standard size should be arranged by an expert cutter or group of cutters, whose business it would be to specialize in that size. When one particular size had been passed in a particular style, foolproof patterns should be prepared for distribution to the workrooms which would eventually be making the garments.

NOTE. The adaptation of a style so as to make it suitable for a larger figure requires emphasis or modification of some of the style points and should be done in consultation with a stylist.'

With an inherent disposition in favour of the carrot rather than the stick, Heron was convinced that participation in the Utility scheme should be voluntary. Accordingly he wrote:

'The original mind behind Utility Clothing.'

'As it is understood to be the Government's intention to leave as much room as possible for individual producers and distributors to apply their enterprise and initiative in their own particular businesses and to retain their identity as firms, it is assumed that the proposed control of styling would not be legally enforceable. But it might be made a condition of Government assistance with regard to supplies of raw materials that these materials should only be used on the approved styles and in the approved sizes. The best use of the Nation's material would thus be secured in the national interest.'

In his conclusion to the Memorandum Heron displayed supreme confidence.

'It is not the purpose of this Memorandum to give detailed proposals, still less to answer all the objections which could be raised to the scheme – this could be attempted when the general principle is accepted. For the moment, the argument is that if the scheme outlined above is put into force, the following benefits will accrue:

1) Fewer designers will be able to do a better job than is at present being done.

2) Fewer pattern cutters will ensure a better cut and sizing than is at present the rule.

3) Fewer power-machinists and hand-sewers will produce more clothes than they would if the trade is left in its present disorganized state.

4) The distribution of clothing will be made much easier than it is at present.

5) The public will certainly get better service from the clothes that are made.

6) The ladies' clothing trade in this country will be organizing itself so as to be able to hold its own in any market after the war.'

Heron's membership of the Economic Reform Club and the Inter-Party Parliamentary Monetary Commission brought him into frequent contact with people who had positions of authority and leadership. One such person, Sir Wilfred Edey, was Minister of Supply at the beginning of the war. Heron arranged to have lunch with Sir Wilfred Edey to put him in the picture. Sir Wilfred told the Board of Trade, of which Oliver Lyttleton was President, that Heron should be put in charge as Director of Civilian Clothing. Heron was summoned to the Board. He was the ideal man for the post. But they had not reckoned with his conscientious objection – shared by his sons. Lyttleton knew that Winston Churchill 'would not wear that.' Whereupon Heron recommended Sir Thomas Barlow for the post and he himself was appointed Adviser on Women's and Children's Clothing, a position he held for four years. What he achieved in that time is unacknowledged to this day, chiefly because of the civil service tradition of anonymity. In reality Heron was the active brain and the original mind and force behind the Utility Clothing Scheme.

One of his first initiatives was to invite London's leading couturiers to his office at the Board of Trade, where he told them that from that moment he wanted them to design 'for the people.' Those present included Norman Hartnell, Hardy Amies, Digby Morton, Edward Molyneux and Bianca Mosca. Thus Heron secured the stylistic pedigree of the Utility Clothing Scheme. Through its success, that scheme became the model for similar Government ventures and when Gordon Russell was asked to organize a similar Utility Furniture Scheme, he consulted Heron over his experience with clothing.

Heron was never a 'civil servant' by nature. Having found on his first morning that at the Board of Trade you do not send your chief assistant out into the street for a box of matches, he quickly learned the rules of the new ball-game and found satisfaction in asserting common sense, but he never changed his spots. In a critical written report on a scheme he had been asked to assess he wrote:

'I am quite certain that facilities for obtaining attractive and durable clothing would prove an inducement to many girls who now resist the Ministry of Labour's efforts to shepherd them where they are wanted. I am convinced that this clothing can, for certain Government employees, be what might be called a uniform, but not uniform. Standardized garments on functional lines can be made by mass production methods in a variety of cheerful colours, which would give the individual an opportunity to choose the colour she wanted. I am sure she would welcome this freedom of choice, and I am sure that a crowd of munition workers dressed in various bright colours and party 'type of clothes' would be a more cheerful sight than a similar crowd dressed in grey or dull blue.'

Years later he enjoyed scrawling across his copy of that document: 'I managed to scotch Mr W's scheme.' The drudgery of daily procedure and detail did not quench Heron's common sense, nor did it wean him from his lifelong pursuit of quality or blinker his vision from wider long-term issues simply to facilitate immediate decisions. He could not forbear to sally forth from the ivory tower of Millbank to join debate on topics engaging public attention. In May 1942 a letter in a *Times* correspondence on quality and postwar exports betrayed a familiar brand of imaginative optimism. 'Is it too much to look forward to the time when the Bond Street dressmaker wears mass-produced gardening slacks whilst the girl who made them has in her wardrobe at least one Bond Street garment individually produced?' It was signed: 'The owner of a plant which has been almost closed down.'

He continued to support the *New English Weekly* but his name had to be deleted from the list of the editorial board and his contributions had to be anonymous. 'I am really very thankful indeed for your most valuable help,' wrote Philip Mairet, adding the reassuring postscript, 'The sheets went to the printer all carefully decapitated.' However, as an employee of the Government, Heron should have taken more care of what he said and wrote and where and when he did so. He caused a great stir when he addressed the National Council of the Pottery Industry in 1943 on Postwar Reconstruction. There were opposite pressures on Heron with regard to this address in particular, and others which he had been giving. There was support for their publication in pamphlet form. There was also pressure from the Board of Trade that there should be no publication. This smacked of suppression! Should Heron resign? What did the Archbishop of Canterbury think? William Temple replied to Heron's question on 14th September 1943:

Utility Suit: London, 1942.

'I am quite unable to judge whether the practical value of the pamphlet would be greater than the practical value of the service you give at the Board of Trade; I am not quite quite sure how much influence you are able to exert there and I therefore cannot make a comparison between the value of your work on the Board and the value of your protest expressed by your resignation. As far as I can judge it is rather absurd that there should be objection raised to the publication, and if there were nothing else to be considered, I should think it right to make the most vigorous protest possible against this. So you will see that I think there would be a real value in the publication and a real value in the resignation. But I must leave it entirely undecided in my own mind whether these outweigh in importance the removal of your influence from the Board itself. I could not take the responsibility of advising one way or the other on that.'

The address was not published as a pamphlet but it was reported fully in the September issue of the *Pottery Gazette and Glass Trade Review* which explained:

'We are giving much space to the address by Mr T.M. Heron because it is one which contains profound thoughts on many angles to be found wherever one considers the post-war position of any industry.'

Heron's address drew on his inside experience of centralized war-time direction of production, some of which, he argued, should continue in peace time. He took advantage of the occasion to illustrate the message of the Archbishop's Malvern Conference in the context of the pottery industry. The following passages from the *Gazette's* report illustrate how he also expounded his personal creed:

'Mr Heron said that by quality was not meant something necessarily costly to produce or highly ornamented. Nor was the distinction between hand-made and machine-made the criterion. Some mass production was quality production and some hand work rubbish.'

'We shall have to discard some of our old machinery, even some of our new, because its use imposes too big a physical strain on the worker.'

'The sign of bureaucracy was the taking of practical decisions that were not practical.'

When it appeared in print there was a flurry of praise and criticism, the former coming from men of such varied experience as the Chairman of Courtaulds, the Staff Manager of Boots and the Chairman of the Institute of Industrial Administration. The *Gazette* gave further space in the next three issues to correspondents' questions along with Heron's answers and comments.

No one knows how close he came to dismissal. Heron continued to work at the Board of Trade till the end of the war and he continued to live dangerously.

Heron's dangers were not simply metaphorical and his guardian angel must have done as much overtime as Heron himself. He had a bed in his office and sometimes stayed in town all week. Reminiscing after the war, he recalled:

'I worked at the Board of Trade sometimes when the bombs were dropping, on two occasions pretty well through the night when we had to get facts and schedules out quickly.'

Eulalie's letters provide a vivid record of life during the onslaught of the flying bombs.

'Daddy was unpleasantly near a crash just a week ago in Mortimer Street, sitting within a yard of an enormous plate-glass window in a restaurant. When one of these fell, the whole window crashed, but into the street, or he must have been seriously hurt.'

One could never tell where the next good night's sleep was to be had. One letter reported:

'You'll be amused and relieved to hear that last time he fire-watched at Westminster Abbey, he insisted on taking his bed into the crypt after his short turn on the roof, and slept soundly from 10 p.m. till 7 a.m. among the colossal Norman pillars and arches.'

On the other hand, Welwyn Garden City was no guaranteed haven. Eulalie again:

'We've had 3 doodle-bug explosions that made us leap out of our beds or bury our heads under the bedclothes according to temperament. One can't stay up all night waiting for the fateful stopping engine, so we try to sleep through these restless nights and manage fairly well except for the big crashes.'

One such crash from a landmine on a nearby chicken farm blew in some of the Herons' windows. Another time a Molotov 'Breadbasket' lit up the woods near the house. Quite apart from the occasional alarums of bombing, home did not always provide the peace that Heron needed. Throughout the war it sheltered a fluctuating company of family, relations, German and Austrian refugees, newly-weds waiting for their own home, conscientious objectors waiting for their tribunals, friends escaping from London and, for a short while, a billetted war-worker. One old family friend stayed almost the whole war. Such a household afforded sociability and stimulation rather than tranquillity.

Once he had acclimatized himself to the Civil Service, and the foundations of the Utility Scheme were laid, Heron began to breath again. Even after an exhausting week at the Board of Trade and a Saturday morning at Cresta, he would somehow find the energy to pursue other interests and responsibilities. Most important were the cogitation and painfully slow reading and writing which were essential to the gestation of a stream of published articles, letters and pamphlets and equally memorable talks, conference addresses and sermons. Eulalie's letter of September 1943 conveys the flavour of this ferment.

'Daddy spoke yesterday afternoon at an important central meeting of the I.C.F. in London. As soon as he'd finished – before discussion – Reckitt jumped up, proposed the speech be published. The Bishop of Bristol seconded – carried.'

And this was the same month as his Pottery address. He was already a school governor and shortly to become churchwarden. It may have surprised his son to receive a paternal letter but not to read in it:

'I've been asked to give an address to Leighton Park School and if your mother doesn't object to my continued week-ends, I shall probably go. This week-end it's Oxford. Next but one Kimbolton. Etc. Etc.'

Heron's mental energy and creativity roamed with increasing freedom as the end of the war approached. In September 1944 he accepted Archbishop Temple's invitation to speak at a weekend conference at Canterbury. The paper was characteristically entitled, 'Co-operation with the Purpose of God in Industry.' When he was finally released from harness to the Board of Trade, the Civil Service ritual of behaviour and idiom was easily and happily shed, but a domestic ritual born of and during the war was retained: the saying of grace at family meals.

Chapter Seven

Post-War Cresta

WAR GAVE WAY TO PEACE but for Heron there was no let-up. On the contrary, the eight years between his release from the Board of Trade in 1945 and his final retirement from full-time work in 1953 witnessed the most protracted and least rewarding struggle of his business career. Many reasons for this lay in the state of the world in general and of commerce in particular. Others derived from the condition and nature of Cresta. Others yet again were peculiar to Heron himself.

A diminishing proportion of the public will remember the post-war world only too clearly. For anyone younger, it may come as a surprise to learn how slowly the disruption and damage of the war was rectified. They will read how

'... rationing and price controls, food subsidies and currency regulations continued long after the end of hostilities and in the critical year of 1947 they became even more severe than they had been during the war itself.'

The expense of making good the damage of bombing and years of neglect, the persisting shortages of goods and services, the cost of the new Welfare State, the military strength required to cope with the 'cold war' besides the real war in Korea – all these factors conspired to prevent taxation dropping back to pre-war levels. Income tax, for example, never more than five shillings in the pound (25%) between 1922 and 1938, was never less than nine shillings in the pound (45%) between 1945 and 1953. Industrial unrest was swollen by Trade Unions' expectations arising from victory in war and a Labour Government after it.

These difficulties were common to all commerce, but the textile industries and their dependent trades had acute problems of their own, compounded by the continuation of clothes rationing until November 1949. The invention of man-made fibres presented manufacturers and users of the traditional materials, wool, cotton and silk, with extremely threatening new rivals at the most vulnerable moment in their history.

This was the climate in which Heron had to throw himself body and soul into the task of reviving Cresta, though the body was ageing and the soul less regularly uplifted by a confident vision of the New Jerusalem and of Cresta's place in it.

As long as the firm remained cramped in its war-time premises within Welwyn Stores, progress was severely limited. There was not even room at first for an office for Heron himself and for several months he worked with his secretary in his own house. So it was cause for rejoicing when it was learned that Cresta's own spacious building would be released by the Government. Eulalie described the party that celebrated the news, the jolly band, the lovely buffet, the marvellous paper hats:

'Everyone was allowed to bring a friend so there were lots of 'boys' but some mothers and fathers too. You should have seen Miss Crump learning the Palais Glide in a jiffy in the middle of a string of eight, while Peter Z followed, very gay, with Daisy Harkett and Miss Roberts on each arm. I suddenly felt Cresta really existed again as a living corporation of friendly people, happy to work together.'

That was in March, 1946. The sequel was written on May 15th.

'This is an important week. Cresta goes back home. The move begins tomorrow night. I've just been over it with Daddy. It looks still quite uninhabitable – an army of workmen still there, painting, sawing, hammering – with newly-painted red CRESTA SILKS lying across the floor of one room, waiting to be erected. Then it looks as if it will need an army of charwomen – two or three poor bodies scrubbing and slopping away would be quite lost in it. And yet Daddy says the move will begin tomorrow, and work, they hope, on Monday.'

Re-establishing its headquarters was the lynch-pin of revival but Heron already had other irons in the fire, to restore the supply of Cresta's famous printed designs and to repair and extend the chain of shops. The situation demanded bold initiatives. Now was the time to fulfil a long-cherished dream and rescue Cryséde, which still possessed property but had virtually ceased activity. Cresta bought a controlling interest in Cryséde's shares, and with it the few remaining shops. The Annual Report of Cresta's Board of Directors covering 1946 reported both the formation of a new Company, Cresta–Cryséde Properties Ltd, and the arrangement of a mortgage of £55,000 to finance it. The memorable print works on 'the island' at St Ives had, alas, been sold years earlier and the Town Council, with its weather eye on tourism, refused to let printing return to the site. Undeterred, Heron found and took over a former biscuit factory in the main square at Hayle at the head of St Ives' Bay to house the resuscitated print-works, and he re-engaged Keith Ross to resume charge of the printing. The original hand-cut wooden blocks were available and for the ensuing six years many of Cresta's designs were printed at Hayle, a new use being found for some of Alec Walker's old Cryséde designs, using totally different colours. After the war Patrick Heron became the chief designer and restored Cresta's avant-garde reputation with some outstanding designs. By this time silk screen printing was increasingly taking over from hand-block printing, so many of Cresta's superb designs were printed by other firms, such as Swaizelands at Deptford and Thomas Wardles, of Leek. It pleased Heron to work with the firm founded by Thomas Wardle, who had helped William Morris learn traditional printing techniques.

Further proof of the vitality of Cresta's revival was provided while the debris of London's bomb damage still lay all around. Seeking to expand his foothold in the West End, Heron secured what came to be regarded as something of a scoop, not least by Irene Date. Recollecting her delight at Heron's return to full-time at Cresta and the acquisition of Cryséde, she continued:

'He also, with great perception and foresight, bought leases and freeholds for several new shops, including a very brave and skilfully negotiated purchase of a shop in Regent St. which produced a remarkable turnover and profit.'

To understand just how brave this was one must realize how slender Cresta's resources were by the end of the war, how uncertain the trading future, and how difficult it was to obtain the licences to repair damage due to enemy action and then to get things done. So work dragged on slowly for months, deferring the opening expected in January 1947 until the following June, and all the time money for its rent had to be found. Nevertheless the Regent Street shop proved a sound venture and seemed a signal of promise that Cresta would mirror, in her post-war revival, her triumphal development out of the economic depression of the early 1930s.

Outwardly that promise was borne out in the next quarter of a century. The name of Cresta became known to an ever wider public, Cresta clothes were made and sold and worn with delight for many years and Cresta employees were made to feel that theirs was a very special company. Only those at the heart of things were aware that the creative pulse was fading. Only with historical hindsight can that decline be properly understood.

In addition to suffering the problems besetting the clothes industry as a whole, Cresta had certain weak spots of its own. As proclaimed by its proper name, 'Cresta Silks', it had been conceived and developed as a firm dealing principally in silk goods. Its economic advantage lay in its independence of middlemen and its ability to guarantee quality by controlling every stage of production from the spindle to the shop. The war put an end to all that. The price of survival had been the abandonment of much of its central policy and practice, though dedication to fine workmanship and familial personal relationships remained. Wool almost entirely replaced silk; bought-in goods bearing little resemblance to those that had made Cresta's reputation provided an essential and growing proportion of its stock.

After the war, it was possible slowly to build up the silk trade again and to increase Cresta's in-house production, but never to its pre-war dominance. What evolved, dictated by circumstances rather than principle, was an element of dualism within the firm. Miss Crump, mainly responsible for creating individual styles, stayed with silk as much as the market would allow, while the bought-in department headed by Irene Date developed its own momentum, mainly dealing with wool and rayon and linked more closely to fashions and trends prevailing outside. It was possible, in such a relatively small firm, to maintain good internal personal relations, but the potential for disagreement and divergence of interests was inescapable and the prolonged depression of the trade made it increasingly difficult to avoid. In particular, it added distinctly to the tension of Heron's rôle as Managing Director. The shop manageresses too had a balancing act to perform. From the customers' point of view, the wider selection of styles and materials was probably an advantage, but in the long run it clearly did not help Cresta re-establish an individual identity.

Contentment and loyalty, especially in the measure enjoyed by Cresta, are a source of cohesion and strength but they can be subject to their own peculiar drawbacks. Almost all of Heron's senior staff had been with him a great many years and they were getting no younger. At a party in January 1952, cheques were presented to seven employees who had completed twenty-one years' service. They knew each other so well that there was a need for fresh ideas and, perhaps, a more critical outlook, fed by experience of other companies' ways of doing things. The Board of Directors was unchanged from 1936 to 1949, and even then it was only to add Irene Date and Muriel Edwards (neé Crump) to their number. It was not surprising to find Heron welcoming women as Directors when most companies remained chauvinist, but it was a sign of rewarding past services rather than importing new blood.

Cresta's failure to provide for the firm's future leadership by recruiting talent of a high order was not due to lack of perception and effort on Heron's part. In particular, he had long been conscious of the importance of finding and training someone to succeed himself. It would have been unnatural in the 1930s for a man with three sons and a daughter not to wonder if they would follow him in the firm he had created in some capacity or other. It would have been equally unnatural for him not to regret later in life that none of them had done so for any length of time. There is a touch of irony in the fact that in the long run, the influence of Heron's belief in personal vocation proved stronger in shaping his children's careers than did his daily business, with which they were all intimately acquainted and felt closely identified. Once again it was the war that determined Cresta's destiny. From the time Patrick was three years old there was no doubt that he would be an artist, so his connection with Cresta, though very significant and spread over almost twenty years, would never have solved the problem of providing Heron with a successor. Even so the war disrupted Patrick's work in designing for Cresta for almost six years.

It was Michael who seemed cut out for a future Managing Director by personality, talent and inclination. After leaving school in 1939, he started in at Cresta with every intention of making it his career and the year he spent there before being called up for national service confirmed Heron in his view that his second son would make a first-class businessman:

'He was always making suggestions and wanting the thing to go quicker than I wanted it to do.'

As with Heron's ideas on vocation, his pacifist creed and example proved a stronger influence than his business. Like Patrick before him, Michael registered as a conscientious objector during the war, as Giles was to do after it. It is not possible to define any causal relationship between Michael's pacifism and his subsequent religious conversion, but the significant fact remains that before he could be released from conscription, Michael's life had taken a permanently different direction and he had found his true vocation as a Benedictine monk. It was therefore an added burden to Heron throughout most of the war to know that the partnership with Michael, to which he had been looking forward eagerly, would not be developed. It proved to be only the first of a series of such disappointments.

It is comparatively easy to find a replacement for a conventional businessman. But the more unorthodox and creative a person has been, the more difficult it is to fill his position. In Heron's case what proved impossible to find was a successor who could combine the commercial ability and experience required to bring Cresta profitably through years of depressed trade with the idealism to preserve and continue his work as an artist and a social reformer. Heron's correspondence shows that the problem was never far from his mind.

After Michael, the most promising person was Patrick's close school friend, Fello Atkinson. As a naval officer stranded ashore at a desk job in New York in 1943, Fello was delighted to receive a copy of Heron's address to the Pottery Industry. That they were on the same wave-length in many matters, is indicated by the comments Fello made on the address.

> 'I am more and more convinced that the machine is the key to our civilization (either for its destruction or its success). If we do not assimilate its spiritual as well as its material possibilities, it will break us.'

In 1944 Heron wrote to ask Fello to join him in Cresta after the war and Fello replied enthusiastically:

> 'Your offer is wonderful. I should love to help and would put my back into it, as there is nothing I should like to do more and no-one I should like to work with more. I accept of course. But first I must warn you that my enthusiasm for buildings has, if anything, increased.'

There is little doubt a Heron-Atkinson partnership would have served Cresta uncommonly well, but the sting in the tail of Fello's response was prophetic. He was to become a distinguished architect. Buildings, not dresses, were his vocation though Heron and Cresta always evoked his interest and affection.

So the search went on. Several men, seriously interested and seriously considered, seemed likely at one time or another to fit the bill. It was a theme constantly recurring in family letters. In 1947 Eulalie wrote optimistically:

> The Hon. Col. Woodhouse is coming into Cresta Silks. I think that is definite now. He went straight to Greece from Oxford and for some years was in the thick of things – then decided it was industry he wants to go for, not politics yet. He has been in Fox Films for a year and is now anxious to serve in Cresta, having been introduced by Dick Reiss. He'll be Daddy's personal assistant.'

Heron himself was necessarily circumspect with regard to Woodhouse. 'He's keen on coming in and I'm trying to find out why he's so keen.' Woodhouse worked closely with Heron for some months and that autumn they were together in Cornwall, where the new Hayle print-works 'was really getting going.' Cresta was charmed by 'Monty.' He recognised and shared Heron's idealism but alas, it did not work out and they parted amicably.

Then there loomed the prospect of Heron's third son Giles entering the business. He was at that time with the French Red Cross, fulfilling his conditional exemption from military service but due for release late in 1948. To help him decide, Heron wondered if he should defer his place at Oxford for a year and try out Cresta first. The idea was set aside only to emerge in another form. In January 1950 Heron wrote to Giles in Oxford before irretrievably offering control to others. Giles was not able to give a clear yea or nay about his own participation.

'You must do the best you can by Cresta and yourself. The burden of feeling obliged to run a firm when I wished to do quite other work would be infinitely heavier than the task of finding another job when Cresta would have suited very well.'

By May 1950 two new candidates had entered the arena. Eulalie monitored progress as usual.

'Daddy's rather weighed down with the big decision he has to make. It's a choice between Crabtree and someone else. Long business talks go on up here – at many of which I'm present – vastly interesting.'

The next letter was more specific about Heron's choice.

'He's still weighing up the pros and cons of Denis N. Its such a big decision to make, nobody else can help him. He was down in Cornwall from Tues. to Sat. with Denis' [Nahum].

Not long after Eulalie was able to describe what was at stake more precisely.

'Daddy is in the throes – it's a choice between C. and N. – endless talks and meetings with all the Directors. Daddy inclines to N. – L.T.M.G. to C. Another dinner at Geoff's place at Canonbury last night. I've been in at a lot of these talks – very interesting. N. is brilliant – but is he stable enough? Cresta's had a bad three months – like all the dress trade – with worse to come almost certainly. Who'll stick it best? I'd back C. to stick it and win through – but he might alter Cresta out of recognition almost in the process of saving it.'

As so often, Eulalie's analysis was spot-on. Heron's excruciating dilemma seemed to be a choice between watching Cresta founder under a sympathetic Nahum or saving it by making a Faustian pact with Crabtree. Heron's whole career had been dedicated to marrying realism with idealism. Now at the last fence, he was facing divorce. The drama had several twists of plot before reaching the inevitable dénouement. In 1951 yet another interested party appeared on the stage, but the scene was comparatively low key. Eulalie once again reports on Heron's progress:

'He isn't actually worrying about the business – and seems to want to forget it when he's at home. The situation hasn't developed in any direction. Mr Darby is here trying it out. He sleeps here from Monday to Friday every week. I don't feed him except breakfast. A nice person.'

Sub-plots delayed the final decision. One concerned the possibility of some form of co-operation or merger with Jaegers. Both firms were hit by the prolonged poor trade. They had long done business together, were similar in being associated with a principal material and selling through their own chain of shops. Obviously Cresta's expertise in silks would be complementary to Jaeger's unrivalled reputation in woollens. Heron and 'Miss Crump' held discussions with Gilbert and others at Jaegers. There was mutual respect between Gilbert and Heron, but not perhaps the easy confidence necessary for a merger to succeed. One bi-product was the arrangement by which Giles, who had 'rather dutifully' – as Heron later described it – decided to enter Cresta, spent ten months on a management training course with Jaegers in Regent Street. Neither aspect bore fruit; Heron and Gilbert judged that they wouldn't succeed together. Giles knew he could never work happily under Crabtree, nor in what he would make of Cresta.

So the saga drew to its end. Heron's successor was to be Eric Crabtree, not his own son Michael or Fello Atkinson, not 'Monty' Woodhouse or Denis Nahum or Robert Darby, not Gilbert or anyone else from Jaegers. Nor was it to be any of Heron's other children, who in each case had enough ability for serious consideration. That Heron didn't totally rule out Joanna is seen in a letter he wrote her in 1948, when she was rather daunted by her teaching practice.

'And if teaching is not your pidgeon (sic) chuck it up! There's plenty of good work for you in Cresta or elsewhere.'

In the event Joanna did 'chuck it up.' An even stronger call led her to sacrifice a promising teaching career and follow parental example, not by entering business but by marrying and rearing four children, whose creative careers illustrate Heron's creed of personal vocation in fruitful operation.

Heron's post-war struggles at Cresta could not but take their toll of his health. He was not often given to complaining, still less to self-pity, so when he found his habitual hopefulness deserting him, he turned in on himself and curled up like a dog. It was only years later, when revived by retirement, that he revealed his real feeling. In 1971 he was able to admit: 'I began to crack up; the strain of the war was greater than I thought.'

There were two distinct periods when the accumulation of worry and fatigue affected his work beyond concealment. In the first it took the form of depression, which developed through 1947 but receded slowly the following year. As might be expected, Eulalie's letters were more informative of his recovery than his developing illness, though there had been earlier hints as in December 1946 when she had written 'Daddy is living at rather high tension just now.' Heron himself let slip an indication of the way the wind was blowing in November 1947, perhaps because he was discussing Giles' career, not his own:

'I simply do not know what Cresta will become. I only know that now there are a hundred worthwhile things I want to do and could give myself to if only time and space didn't impose their limitations.'

Soon after, an invitation to Yorkshire that would normally have been welcomed had to be turned down. 'Tom is too tired to travel to Crambe for Christmas.' Early in 1948 Eulalie was more explicit:

'He's been completely tired out – to the point of exhaustion – and kept staying in bed for breakfast.'

By April, however, the tide had turned as Joanna was able to tell Giles:

'You'll be glad to hear Daddy is a great deal better. He feels quite different – interested in things and with a sense of humour and optimism.' Eulalie added: 'The great depression has gone. He feels like himself.'

Recovery of spirit, however, did not in itself solve the problems that had caused the depression; they found another outlet instead. After a family holiday in the Lake District in 1950, Heron's knees began to cause him trouble and they got worse as 1951 progressed. His predicament was captured in the invaluable reminiscence recorded by his granddaughter Katharine:

'For a time I couldn't walk a mile. Later I couldn't walk ten yards. I remember getting the telephone company to put an extension in my bedroom and for some weeks I carried on by telephone to the various people in the business and by their coming up to see me.'

In April the consultant diagnosed osteo-arthritis. He must rest as much as possible for three months and must avoid walking. Rest and warmth were the only cure. So Heron and Eulalie went to Sorrento. His stay there marked the nadir of his post-war business career. Baking in the Italian sun, he was reduced to unwonted idleness and dependence. There is a photo of him being carried in a sedan chair, red as a lobster. 'Eventually,' he recalled, 'I sort of crawled back to Cresta.' Before the year was out his knees were mending, but destiny was already beginning to take Cresta out of his hands.

Other factors had also contributed to Heron's depression. One was the demise of the *New English Weekly*, from the closure of which he lost both inspiration and a pulpit – or a soap box! Always run on a shoestring, the journal was remarkable for its survival rather than its mortality. Pulling out of a trough of confidence in 1948, Heron busied himself re-establishing contact with his old school friend, Eric (Peter) Gregory of Lund Humphries in an eleventh-hour attempt at salvage, but the paper folded quietly in 1949.

One of the lesser factors contributing to Heron's depression had been the compulsory take-over of Welwyn Garden City by the Labour Government, abruptly ending the idealistic enterprise nurtured by men who had become his close friends.

The new settlement involved the creation of a Development Corporation to complete the development of the town and of the Howardsgate Trust to administer some of the assets of the redundant Welwyn Garden City Company, including its subsidiary businesses, notably Welwyn Stores. John Eccles, the Managing Director of both the Trust and Welwyn Stores, had been a Cresta Director since 1935. His ebullient optimism swept the convalescent Heron into an arrangement which hit the headlines of the *Welwyn Times* on Sept. 21st 1951: 'The Company Buys Control of Cresta.' While reporting that Heron and the existing Directors would remain in place, the paper explained that the change was expected to result, the following year, in substantial development and expansion. In itself the change of ownership did not immediately alter either Cresta's goods or the lives of her employees, but it opened the door to a larger, less personal, scale of business. The stage was set for the transition from Cresta under Heron, in whom the desire for quality burned more ardently than the need for dividends, to Cresta under Crabtree, of whom the obituary in the *Independent* was to say that 'nothing gave him as much pleasure and excitement as a deal carried to profitable success.'

Eric Crabtree eventually joined Cresta in the spring of 1952 and for a while the two men worked together. An exceptional fruit of the brief period of their collaboration was the celebrated Coronation scarf. Heron went to Switzerland to arrange for Oliver Messel's etherial design – with its royal emblems and fairy coach – to be printed by a pioneering technique using real gold. The scarf appeared on the front cover of the fashion magazine *Vogue*, with a full-page editorial about its design and its printers. Heron's pride overcame his discretion when encouraging his shop manageresses to promote it.

> 'I tell you in confidence that the Queen, the Queen Mother, the Duchess of Kent and Princess Margaret have all accepted scarves, and said very nice things about them too!'

It was Heron's brilliant final creative fling in business.

On September 30th, 1953 Eulalie was thankful to be able to write:

> 'I feel that Daddy's retirement has really begun this week.'

Outwardly all was well. Retirement for Heron; business as usual for Cresta. The family feared otherwise. 'Have you seen the new Cresta collection? Not a single Cresta print!' The writing was already on the wall. The Hayle works was closed and the wooden printing blocks burnt. The headquarters building was sold, as factory, offices and shop moved back into Welwyn Stores, where the machinists worked behind blacked-out windows to appease the town's planning policy. Almost all traces of Wells Coates were removed from the original shops, in favour of Regency pastiche – 'We're not in building we're in fashion!' Cresta was bought by Debenhams, and all the while turnover and dividends magnified. In terms of his own priorities, still predominant as the century closed, Crabtree was a brilliant success. By 1973 there were more than eighty shops and over eleven hundred employees. But to Heron 'it felt like failure', as Eulalie put it. It took a crisis of a different sort to make Heron show his inner feelings. When Eulalie was having an inexplicably grim time in hospital in 1959, he sought to share the blame.

'It may be that my lack of masculinity, which made me make a muck of Cresta, played havoc with you.'

Heron's unexpected phrase of self-criticism was as unjust as if Don Quixote blamed himself for failing to knock down windmills. What was remarkable was not the fact that no successor emerged capable of maintaining Heron's balance between the ideal and the worldly, but the degree to which his vision had materialized in the first place. Cresta itself was a work of art akin to the performance arts which live and germinate in the memory, not as artefacts in museums. Though its tradition of hand-printing was an early casualty of Heron's retirement, many valuable aspects of his legacy continued to inspire Cresta's employees and customers for at least two further decades, as is shown in the testimony of Helen Hamlyn, the designer. All her fifteen years at Cresta were under Crabtree, whom she regarded as the world's greatest salesman, yet her description of the firm she had been desperately keen to work for and in which she stayed till her marriage, was in most respects the firm of Heron's creation and vision.

'People who really knew about making good clothes at relatively low costs. It started with the right ideas. Its spirit was right. Everybody cared about doing things properly. It was unique, absolutely unique in this country and in the fashion world to have somewhere like Cresta.'

Chapter Eight

Welwyn Garden City

IT IS A REASONABLE OPINION that the early history of Welwyn Garden City provides the most successful example of town planning and community development in Britain in the twentieth century. The fortunate resident of Ebenezer Howard's second Garden City was to live in a well-built, cottage-style house, with its own gardens among avenues of flowering trees set in grass verges safely separating the pavement from the roadways. A mere five or ten minutes' walk in one direction would bring him to the edge of open country and the great stretch of open woodland, or more recent pine plantations, where he was free to roam. Such briefly was the garden. The city element comprised a more formal civic centre complete with shops and services, schools, libraries, theatres and churches and all manner of sports facilities. Beyond, to leeward, lay the industrial area, only another few minutes' walk.

> 'The town invaded the country but the invaders yielded to the influence of their surroundings and became country people. So the difference between town and country grew less and less and was, indeed, the world of the country vivified by the thought and briskness of town-bred folk which had produced that happy and leisurely but eager life.'

The above passage, which could be mistaken as coming from a history of one of Howard's Garden Cities, is in fact imaginative fiction written in 1890 and it fascinated Tom Heron as a young man. Although he deliberately forewent university education in his impatience to enter the real world of business, he read avidly wherever his instinct led him. And since his instinct led him on a life-long quest to marry the practical organization of society with idealism, he discovered and devoured the ideas of More's *Utopia*, Robert Owen's *New Lanark* and William Morris's *News From Nowhere*, the last of which contains our quotation.

When Heron was on a business visit to London in 1918, that instinct led him to attend a meeting about Howard's campaign to create a successor to the first Garden City, established at Letchworth in 1903. The speaker was R.L. Reiss, who was about to act as midwife to Welwyn Garden City, where Heron was to live for most of the rest of his life. That settled period was still far off and the first ten years of his marriage and family-raising were to take place in the dramatically contrasting environments of Leeds and the Cornish Riviera, but the seed of Heron's devotion to the Garden City ideal had been sown and awaited its due season.

It was no mere chance therefore that in 1929, when faced with the necessity of choosing somewhere to start up an entirely new business and to bring up their

Welwyn Garden City: a typical street scene.

A greetings card from the Heron family (Patrick Heron c. 1934).

family of four, the Herons should have turned to Welwyn Garden City. They were both excited by the prospect of joining an idealistic community in its formative stages. It would help to obliterate their Crysède experience. From London Tom reported progress on his searches:

'Just back from Welwyn. It's good to be alive. I am going to have my chance. I like the air of Welwyn and I think I can do my bit towards moulding it. I am just ready for it and it is just ready for me. When I saw it four years ago, it was a wilderness – so uncreated that I, in my idealistic state, would have tried the impossible on it. Now I am practical and it has just got itself easily established.'

Catching his enthusiasm, Eulalie wrote back from Cornwall: 'If we go there you will be one of the future builders of the town, I guess.' A prophecy amply borne out during the next half century.

Eulalie's very considerable contribution to Welwyn Garden City, like so much of her life, escapes or defies description, partly because its core was expressed in personal, one-to-one relationships. By contrast, Heron rarely went unnoticed. The combination of his extraordinary energy, self-confidence and organizing ability was emphasized by his striking appearance, his tall erect figure and dark, Shavian beard. He was a natural choice for the second edition of *Who's Who in Welwyn*, a popular publication helping to create interest and a corporate identity among the early residents, accompanying brief summaries of the achievements of prominent citizens with witty pen-and-ink sketches.

Naturally, Heron's greatest contribution to his new community was the creation of Cresta Silks, bringing employment, talent and trade to the town and helping to put it on the map throughout the country as the firm established its high reputation. But while Cresta began to prosper, Heron never forgot or neglected his commitment to the less fortunate, especially exploited workers and the unemployed. When six redundant miners from South Wales came singing and begging outside their home in Valley Road, the Herons agreed with the Welsh M.P., Mr Cove and his wife, who lived opposite, to invite them in to share their week-end joints; three to each house.

Of much more significance was the initiative Heron took to alleviate the demoralization and restore the self-respect of the unemployed in his new community. The front-page news of the *Welwyn Times* of September 8th 1932 included the following:

'Mr T.M. Heron, Managing Director of Cresta Silks Ltd, who is actively interested in the unemployment problem, addressed a meeting of local unemployed men outside Bridge Road East Labour Exchange on Friday morning last. He told them he was afraid that unemployment was not likely to improve. He had, during the last month or so, travelled considerably over England and he was forced more and more to the conclusion that the first step in the solution of the problem was for them to help themselves and that it was of little use waiting for the politicians and economists to give them the lead. As an instance of the self-help movement, he mentioned that the unemployed in Cornwall were sending quantities of herrings and other fish up to Leeds for the unemployed there, who in return were sending clothing down to Cornwall.'

Much of the rest of the report dealt with the particular project of self-help Heron was trying to promote, the building of 'an unemployed hut,' to be a sort of clubhouse for the recreation of the unemployed. An important part of the therapy was that the unemployed were to build and administer it themselves. Heron's business contacts and powers of persuasion helped to secure gifts of money and raw materials and the hut was built, thoughtfully sited next to the Labour Exchange.

Heron's pragmatic radicalism met with more appreciation and co-operation in Welwyn's business circles than would have been likely elsewhere, which accounts in part for the number and effectiveness of many of his initiatives. He became a prominent Rotarian and took his turn as President (1934–5). He also took part in a scheme which raised funds and gave Jarrow families a holiday in the Garden City. Certain generous residents, when going away on holiday themselves, allowed their homes to be occupied by Jarrow families (who slept on straw pallets) while others looked after the visitors and laid on trips and entertainments such as treasure-hunts, organized sports and dancing. An extra benefit arising from this scheme was that some people from Jarrow were able to settle in Welwyn Garden City permanently, having found jobs in its companies, one of which was Cresta.

However the fertility and optimism of Heron's mind threw out more ideas than he could ever have time to see through to fruition, as the *Welwyn Times* frequently bore witness.

'A suggestion that the country should be run as "Great Britain Ltd". was voiced by Mr T.M. Heron when addressing the local Fabian Society last Sunday on the subject of "Economic Nationalism", March 9th, 1933.

'A scheme for a Market House for Welwyn Garden City was suggested by Mr T.M. Heron at a meeting of the Consumer Money League. It would be designed not only to assist producers of all kinds of goods, but to provide a working experiment in a new currency system ... The scheme would be in essence a form of scientific barter.' July 12th, 1934.

'A most entertaining lecture on the possibility of a leisured state in the future was given by Mr T.M. Heron at the Arts Club on Saturday night,' March 14th 1934.

Heron also enlivened the *Welwyn Times* with his letters. One in October 1934 publicized a communal hot-water supply in the Midlands. This letter concluded:

'Now Welwyn Garden City is noted for its up-to-date housing schemes and for its heating engineers. A new housing scheme is at the present moment under consideration by the Urban District Council. If a communal hot-water supply is now a practical proposition, surely we in Welwyn Garden City ought to be one of the first communities to have one.'

Another letter, appearing on May 31st the same year, included the following characteristic remarks:

'Sir, Walking down Bond St. yesterday afternoon I was attracted by a box of cigars displayed in a tobacconist's window. A closer inspection revealed the price to be 75 gns per 100. Now I have a soft corner in my heart for the connoisseur ... At the moment, however, those cigars have left a bad taste in my mouth. For today's *Manchester Guardian* contains a report on an investigation at Newcastle-upon-Tyne ... Briefly the result is that in those cases where working-class mothers are expected to feed and clothe a child for two months at the cost of one of those cigars, with regard to anaemia only 20% passed the satisfactory test.'

He was still provocative in February 1938 and sparked off an extended correspondence when suggesting that the letters clergy had contributed to the paper about a case of an employee's summary dismissal should be used as texts for their sermons in church, where they should be followed by discussion by both employers and employees.

Heron's great appetite for the drama of real life was fed by his enjoyment of his own rôles in many spheres. Eulalie loved acting: they both liked the sociability of amateur dramatics and were glad to host play-reading evenings in their home. But Heron himself was a bad actor because he was always himself. To make matters worse, he could never remember his lines, which explains why he had been relegated to the lion's part when a Fabian summer school passed a rainy afternoon over Shaw's as yet unpublished *Androcles and the Lion*. 'No, Heron!' Shaw protested, 'I prefer my words to yours.' So it is surprising to find that he was at one time Chairman of the Welwyn Drama Club. He always maintained he owed it to the fact that all the other possible candidates wanted office in order to be able to cast their wives in leading rôles. For several decades, the annual Welwyn Drama Festival week was one of the highlights of their year. It is typical not only of Heron's self-confidence, but also of other people's confidence in him, that when the professional adjudicator was suddenly taken ill, nobody but he could be persuaded to take over at a moment's notice.

Indeed Heron took an interest in most aspects of the town's life and was always ready to help. When he heard that the town band couldn't play because their instruments were in pawn, he set about getting support which returned the instruments to the players and the band to the streets – though secretly Eulalie had preferred the silence.

He was one among many vice-presidents of the Welwyn Rugby Football Club and was often, business permitting, on the touchline during their games, not just when his sons were playing. It was one of the proudest moments of his paternal life when Michael played in the St George's Harpenden team that won the first-ever Public Schools' Seven-a-Side Tournament.

Back in Cornwall in 1929, Eulalie had guessed that her husband would become 'one of the future builders of the town.' Apart from the major contribution of Cresta, the picture emerging so far is of a prominent, colourful and independent-minded citizen. In 1968 an old lady he didn't know came up to him and said, 'Everything's changed since I came to the Garden City in '35. You're the only thing that hasn't changed.' He was someone too with a reputation for compassion, to whom a desperate man could turn for help when his wife had shaken the crumbs off the supper table into the fire and with them his week's wages. If Eulalie's greater expectation was justified, it was by the important work Heron dedicated to Sherrardswood School (known as the High School until 1938), and to St Francis' Church, in each case over a period of thirty to forty years.

Sherrardswood School

THERE IS SOMETHING OF A PARADOX in the fact that a man who spent so much of his time and energy spreading ideas and assisting educational institutions, indeed a man from whom people learned so much, should signally lack the talents of a teacher. As Eulalie observed:

'A good teacher has to start from where a pupil is.
Tom starts by telling them what he wants them to know.'

Like Dickens' Mr Podsnap, he tended to repeat more loudly what had not been understood. He was at his best in impromptu debate or before an audience that was eager to follow a trail he had blazed.

As social reformers and admirers of Morris and Ruskin – and in Tom's case of Edward Carpenter too – the Herons were naturally sympathetic towards the Progressive School Movement in its early, moderate phase. They were delighted to find on arrival in the town in 1929, that such a school was being established. Patrick and Michael were enrolled at once and Joanna and Giles followed as they reached school age. Tom and Eulalie became enthusiastic members of the Parents' Association.

That Eulalie was a teacher by nature and experience is illustrated by this passage from the appreciation she wrote in the *Welwyn Times* when Joy Wragg, the founding Headmistress, retired:

'As for the children, I should not claim that they are better informed or better behaved or more industrious than other children. But one or two things I do claim. They are actively happy in their school work and life. They enjoy it. They are alert and keen, learning to work by themselves, each at his or her rate of progress, and so becoming independent. They are self-confident; fears seem to have been banished because each child finds there is something it can do well.'

In contrast, Heron's contribution to Sherrardswood was the fruit of the unstinting efforts by which he harnessed his business acumen and powers of leadership. It sprang from his conviction that this was the best sort of education and that Welwyn Garden City had a particular need of it.

Writing in her autobiography years later in 1967, Joy Wragg concluded:

'Mr Heron has done more, perhaps, than anyone else to help the school achieve and maintain its present status.'

She remembered clearly a staff meeting held over thirty years before in the Herons' house, when Heron offered the views of the 'forward-looking businessman':

'Our present difficulties are not due to monetary maladjustments, tariffs, over-production or under-consumption. These are only symptoms of a social order dominated by greed and fear. As soon as we have learned to co-operate and love, so soon shall we live in an era of plenty.

'We must therefore be very careful not to fill our children's heads with ideas about party or class. Conservatism, liberalism, socialism, capital, labour – they are old-fashioned already. Let us direct their energies to the understanding of co-operative effort, by clear thinking and a loving heart, which brings us to the moral and spiritual training – the necessary background to material understanding.'

Miss Wragg also wrote:

'Mr and Mrs Heron sensed that the school would increase much as a living organism grows naturally and wholesomely if given the chance.'

This provides a clue to a second paradox regarding Heron and education, that so radical a reformer and champion of the underdog should be so dedicated to the creation and survival of a private school. The answer is complex for Heron crusaded on many fronts. Though he disliked privilege, he mistrusted uniformity. Monopoly and bureaucracy roused his defiance. The institutions he served – businesses, churches, schools and looser groups – were organic associations of individuals. Above all, he was pragmatic not doctrinaire in his consistent pursuit of quality.

The Herons did not desire boarding school education for their children, nor could they afford it, but at the time Patrick reached the age of twelve, the school had not developed any senior classes nor was there yet any secondary education in Welwyn Garden City. As a result he was sent to St George's School in Harpenden, six miles away, followed by Michael and Joanna. It was one of the very few co-educational boarding schools at that time. Abbotsholme, the forerunner of Bedales and Gordonstoun, was thought more suitable for Giles. In each case the financial support of a scholarship was essential.

Many well-established independent schools were casualties of the war, of the post-war period of austerity, and of the Labour Government's hostility to the private sector. For Sherrardswood the situation was particularly precarious since neither the town nor the school was fully developed when war broke out. Its survival was principally due to Jim and Moira Annand, who had bought the school in 1935 and ran it until 1947. But they needed much help, especially in matters of finance, legal constitution and public relations. Heron, who had been Chairman of the Parents' Association, was a member of the Advisory Council which the Annands set up in 1939 and which became a formal Board of Governors in 1941, when Sherrardswood became a limited company with charitable status.

Once Heron was committed to the Board of Trade, the time he could devote to the school's affairs was considerably restricted, but he had already played a leading part in an ambitious scheme. In the dark days between Dunkirk and the Battle of Britain, plans were begun to evacuate all the school's pupils to the safety of the United States together with a number of mothers. Despite much trepidation, Eulalie was prepared to accompany Joanna and Giles and like all of the Sherrardswood party, had been allocated to a specific host or fostering family in Massachusetts. With the prospect of a long separation, the family posed for uncharacteristically formal photographs, which still betray the dramatic seriousness of that wartime moment. For the Heron family that separation never materialized. Changes of regulations by the Governments on both sides of the Atlantic reduced the scheme to a shadow of its original substance and the party that finally sailed in August 1940 comprised only twenty-six pupils and two mothers.

The approach of the end of the war promised Heron more time, so when in 1945 his friend and colleague John Eccles retired as Chairman of the Governors of Sherrardswood, Heron took his place. Remarkable to relate, he remained Chairman until 1971, serving five successive headmasters, so the story of his work for Sherrardswood overlaps considerably with the story of the school itself, especially during the twenty-six adventurous, and occasionally turbulent, years under his chairmanship. Probably he should have retired much earlier, but it is easy to be wise after the event and it is a measure of his stature that others were reluctant to take over. An interesting perspective comes from the bank manager, Michael Gambling, who ultimately succeeded Heron, having only known him as a septuagenarian:

> 'He was, I felt, an optimist insofar as he always pressed for expansion and bold policies, notwithstanding that the school had no endowment or income other than fees, and a small educational establishment in the private sector did not command much credit.
>
> 'He had undoubtedly a personality which helped to found the school in its early days and to take it through more than one crisis – mainly financial I believe – to stability.'

There were indeed several crises when the closure of the school seemed likely if not inevitable and they weighed all the more heavily on Heron because the political and economic conditions that precipitated them also threatened his other commitments, notably Cresta and the *New English Weekly*. If these crises were usually financial in origin, their solution required educational vision, courage and opportunism. The most important achievement was the establishment of boarding houses. Heron's influence was felt not just in reaching the policy decision that boarding provision would best solve the financial shortcoming, but also in obtaining leases first on Digswell Park House and later on Lockleys, and then in scraping together the necessary money.

Perhaps the aspect of his achievement which no-one else would have been able to match was his providing the vital link between Sherrardswood and the sources of local financial support on which the school increasingly depended, the Welwyn Garden City Company and other leading commercial and industrial bodies. As usual, Eulalie maintained the family's bush telegraph:

'Meanwhile Daddy lunches with a covey of managers – anyway something suggesting a nest he intends to rob on behalf of Sherrardswood – ICI – Norton's – de Haviland – Murphy and so on. He doesn't leave a stone unturned – he even hacks up the pavement.'

Less subjective, if more prosaic, observers were nevertheless very appreciative and complimentary. The jubilee record of the school's first fifty years includes the testimony of Jack Eastwood, Headmaster from 1947 to 1953.

'Our determination to succeed was strengthened by the encouragement given to us from the very beginning by Tom Heron, surely one of the most remarkable men in the school's history. To us personally he showed the very greatest kindness and consideration throughout our six years' tenure of office, and for his confidence, enthusiasm and sound judgement over a much longer period than that, I feel the school owes him a tremendous debt of gratitude.'

St Francis' Church

TOM AND EULALIE WERE GUESTS OF HONOUR at a memorable Eucharist at St Francis' Church one Sunday morning in late September 1978. Since the occasion marked both their diamond wedding and the end of their forty-nine years' residence in Welwyn Garden City, the service combined congratulations and thanksgiving and a concluding ceremony with the couple enthroned in a side aisle to allow departing members of the congregation to make their personal farewells and, in many cases, bestow floral and other tributes.

What lay behind this rare and moving event? Doubtless other parishioners attended more regularly, held office longer or performed more duties, but 'Tom and Jack' – as most would have thought of them – had come to occupy a very special place in the hearts and minds of several generations of the St Francis' congregation. They were valued even more for who they were than for what they did, remarkable though that was. What they meant to their fellow worshippers can best be described in their own words, mostly written in 1981, beginning with Betty Speaight's memories of Tom:

'Perhaps what made most impression on me was his true kindness, which extended beyond feelings of compassion and expressed itself in practical help. I know of many unfortunate and insignificant persons whom the world might not have troubled about, who must have reason to thank Tom and Eulalie for their compassion and practical help.'

This last trait is illustrated by Canon Norfolk, who succeeded as Vicar in 1959. Norfolk said he regarded Heron as an elder statesman.

'He helped to teach me the importance of learning to love God with all one's mind, while his deep humanity and his interest in the arts always demonstrated that this could never be a merely cerebral activity.

'I think of Tom Heron as a man generous in disposition and action. I know of one particular matter where he replaced some misappropriated funds at considerable cost to himself and also gave considerable help and support to the man responsible.'

Gladys Keable fills in the emerging portrait:

'Tom is paterfamilias, whether of his own immediate family, or of the families of his in-laws, or of any group he belonged to, or of his local church; and his home and family were available for any members of these groups, perhaps more particularly for anyone that had gifts that could be encouraged, or shortcomings that needed help.'

After remembering how Heron 'worshipped and enjoyed the abundance of life and all life forces,' David Bowes added another vivid thumb-nail sketch:

'His admiration for courage, perseverance, endeavour, ingenuity and enterprise was unbounded; equally his total dismissal and condemnation of cant, opportunism, self-indulgence, shallow plausibility and waste were unremitting – and yet always these aberrations and weaknesses and not the man himself were his target; a man in his eyes could always find redemption and be forgiven,'

Which explains the surprised admiration of Ellen Bell:

'They'd help anybody, Germans or whoever came to the door. He's even taken tramps in, given them food, cheese, anything available. He'd give them a good feed and once he took a man in to do his gardening that had just come out of prison.'

Besides the countless individuals welcomed into their homes on Brockswood Lane, the Herons extended their hospitality to a variety of groups associated more or less closely with the Church, from the traditional Prayer and Bible groups, through less common Fellowship or Industrial groups, to the most ambitious of all, Tom's Science Group, which played so important a part in his retirement years that it is covered separately in a later chapter.

Over the years, the Herons' Church allegiance involved them in a great many and widely varied activities, such as these Fellowship meetings in 1947, recorded in Eulalie's family letters. On a June evening over twenty turned up for a treasure hunt in the Herons' garden, followed, after refreshment, by singing round the piano. In November Tom took the chair for a talk by the Garden City architect Louis de Soissons on 'The present building and future plans of the Church.' Eulalie wrote:

'He spoke as a man does who cares about a place of worship and its purpose.' The next month Eulalie was writing: 'I am running the Fellowship meeting on Wednesday, Xmas readings, carols and games.'

Somehow Heron managed to dovetail his periods of greatest activity in Church affairs with his efforts to cope with overlapping crises in his other commitments, notably Cresta, Sherrardswood and the *New English Weekly*. Possibly these different spheres were essential to each other. In any case, his interest and involvement in public life continued unabated and though many events are now forgotten, those that surface in letters and diaries serve to indicate the rest. In the autumn of 1947 he spoke at Woodford Congregational Chapel and at a London church in the same week. At this time he was already Churchwarden at St Francis' and in the following February he was appointed the lay member of a commission of three to hold an inspection of a theological college at Cheshunt along with the Bishop and Dean of St Alban's. This was not to be his only contact with the Bishop that year. The interregnum in 1948 following the Rev. Arthur Watkins' retirement produced a dilemma which Heron solved with characteristic boldness. The P.C.C. were convinced that the man the Bishop had decided to appoint was entirely unsuitable for their particular parish. Alerted to recent legislation by his learned friend Demant, Heron arranged with the P.C.C. that the two Churchwardens should present their case at a formal meeting at St Albans and inform the Bishop that they would exercise their new right to refuse to accept the Bishop's nominee for six months. 'They fought firmly and gently for over an hour – and they won!' Eulalie reported. 'I feel in a way it was a triumph for the Bishop too, because he does stand on his authority but he was willing to give way. That's what Christian negotiation should be.' Instead the Bishop appointed Geoffrey Keable, whom Heron knew and had supported. St Francis' was to owe a great deal to the guidance and inspiration of Geoffrey and his wife Gladys over the next decade, as it developed into the lively and adventurous congregation that seemed both the peculiar need and the natural product of a pioneer town such as Welwyn Garden City.

In May 1949 Heron preached in Southwark Cathedral on 'What has Christianity to say on leisure in the modern state?' In May 1952 we find him organizing an Industrial Sunday meeting at the Community Centre Welwyn Garden City, to be addressed by Sir Wilfred Garrett, a colleague of his on the Christian Frontier Council.

'All is too much!' The exclamation which opens a poem Heron was to write years after could well have expressed his turmoil before he was finally freed from the grind of daily business in 1953. It was only to be expected that under the combined weight of his responsibilities, those he had chosen himself and those constantly thrust upon him, he could not always live up to his own high standards. Eulalie's honesty matched her concern and would not conceal disappointments when they came. So she referred to:

'the second symposium here on Sunday evening led by Daddy, who was tired, and it didn't go too well. Still we're beginning to see what we can usefully do. We are reading Dorothy Sayers' *Why Work?*

The seeds of the future Science Group were being sown.

Heron's resignation as Churchwarden effected only a limited diminution of his activity, but it permitted him to range more freely in both religious and secular fields. In 1959 he learned that his successors as Churchwarden had scraped together fifty pounds towards the Keables' much needed holiday. Eulalie takes up the tale:

'Then Daddy got hold of it of course and in a few days he'd got £25 from I.C.I., £25 from*, £25 from** and so on. So that at the A.G.M. last Monday we were able to give them a cheque for £325, which meant that instead of sitting at Dover, they flew yesterday to the Mediterranean.'

Nature, nurture and adult experience all conspired to make the Herons sympathetic towards ecumenical developments. Their son Michael's decision to become first a Roman Catholic and then a Benedictine monk only served to strengthen an existing inclination, so that Eulalie's letter to her daughter Joanna in 1966 came as no surprise:

'We are very much pre-occupied with the services for unity held in the different churches. We went almost every evening to the half-hours of prayer and sometimes to the fifteen minutes lunchtime ones.'

Early the following year another initiative was being described:

'Perhaps you haven't heard of the People-next-Door campaign which churches are taking up all over the country. For us it means that every week for six or seven weeks we have a group of people here – none of whom we know – 11 of them – and they include an R.C. Trade Unionist, an elderly Methodist lay-preacher, two couples from the Free Church, a woman teacher and another welfare worker. There are over 300 people in Welwyn all doing this in groups.

'And mixed up with all this has been the week of Prayer for Unity with various services going on. It started with evensong at St Francis', to which many R.C. s came. We had an R.C. Preacher Jesuit, Father Corbishley, whom Tom got to come – a splendid man!'

Heron was ready to share his experience and his thinking with anyone who seemed genuinely interested. A school friend coming to stay with Giles was deeply impressed by him:

'I used to think of him as God. Not because he looked like the stained-glass image but because of his prophetic pronouncements backed by much reading and thought. What I found particularly inspiring and exciting was his willingness to discuss politics and theology with a fourteen year-old. It was through the Herons that I, from a liberal agnostic background, became persuaded that Christianity could be reconciled with reason.'

This ability of Heron's to relate to adolescents on a serious level naturally extended to St Francis', where at parish breakfast he could often be seen nodding thoughtfully as he listened to the more youthful. His age was almost an asset rather than a barrier. Eulalie wrote the following just before his eightieth birthday:

'Daddy (and I) went to church on Sunday evening for him to talk to the new teen-age club that has recently got going. Usually they play ping-pong, drink coffee, and then someone talks about something. They've kept off religious subjects and serious discussion so far, deliberately, but of course nothing else was of interest to Daddy. He did it very well. His opening proposition to them was that none of them could expect to go through life without meeting some misfortune or serious difficulty. How did they think they would cope with it? They didn't object in the end to the mention of God.'

At the age of seventy-seven Heron remained true to his personal optimistic brand of Christian philosophy. Convinced as ever that God always matched the Church's opportunities to its responsibilities, he was possessed of a vision and an enthusiasm reminiscent of his prime. In this instance he saw that the parish's duty to complete the building of its own church and its social obligation to the wider community could share a common solution. He aimed to kill two birds with one stone, the stone being his proposal to set up a Housing Association and to sell it some of the surplus land behind the church on which it would build sheltered accommodation for the elderly, thus providing money towards the completion of the church. Not content with tossing his stone into the P.C.C. pond and watching the ripples, he couldn't refrain from plunging into detailed consideration of the host of problems that his proposal uncovered, for, as in the case of true love, the course of development on consecrated land never did run smooth.

Heron's energy was remarkable. He played a leading part in the committees set up to progress the scheme, worked over plans and drawings with the architect, visited potential residents and discussed their needs with the people running the '65 Club.' Even his most practical and cautious critic – partly given to playing devil's advocate – was generous in praise. 'I fully understand your point of view and admire the drive and tenacity with which you are putting over your most valuable scheme.'

Many people were attracted to the project; others doubted or were daunted as complications multiplied. Faced with the unending succession of difficulties raised by such authorities as the Charity Commissioners, the National Housing Association, the Church Hall Trustees and the Diocesan Legal Secretary, in addition to all the usual planning, building and car-parking regulations, even supporters began to run out of steam. After a year of urgent bustle throughout 1967, the parish found itself heading for a quiet backwater with the prize still out of reach.

Like a dog with a bone, Heron would not let go of his vision; no more would his brain-child lie down and die. In 1971 it re-surfaced and Heron showed that he still had a contribution to make, as the faithful chronicler Eulalie informed the family that October:

'Daddy is speaking to the Campus Group here – about 100 Garden Citizens – men only – on Thursday. He's going to try to get them interested in the Old People's Flats idea at the Church, which has revived and is being taken up realistically. He wants it to include an Old People's Club – with a canteen – to keep open every day instead of just one afternoon as at present. And today we are going with David Sutcliffe (who is architect to the scheme) to have lunch at the Old People's Centre at Hatfield, which he thinks is excellent.'

So the struggle continued, until it came to fruition shortly before the Herons left the Garden City for the Lake District. Contacts with St Francis' were maintained by many correspondents, of whom one, Hilda Davidson, wrote rejoicing in 1980:

'I have seen Betty and have visited Dorothy Scofield's new flat – it is wonderful how Tom's scheme all those years ago for the flats for older people has worked out, and how good they are.'

We have met Betty already. After hearing of Heron's death in 1983, she was to write:

'I always felt he was one of those comparatively rare persons who looked upon death as an entry into a world to which he had lived very near during his life on earth.'

Chapter Nine

Money and the Just Price: Chandos

ONE OF HERON'S NOTABLE TRAITS was his ability to bridge the gulfs between disciplines and spheres of activity which left most people stranded on one side or the other. This was very marked in relation to monetary policy and finance. His booklet, *Christian Vocation in Industry and Marketing*, published in 1926, opened with two quotations. One was from Adam Smith's *Wealth of Nations* and the other was the verse from St Matthew's Gospel: 'Seek ye first the Kingdom of God and all these things shall be added unto you.' Heron's attitude to money was rooted firmly in both. His achievement was to accommodate both in his own life and work.

Money had always been of interest to Heron quite apart from its acquisition – which was often elusive. 'In the family we don't need money to distribute what is on the breakfast table.' As usual his thought and expression were individual.

'God did not create money. It does not grow on a tree, nor is it found in the ground like ore. Money is something which men have made in order that they may the better accomplish some human purpose; and money is to be judged in the same way as other things which men have made, by its RESULTS.'

Heron's constant theme was that the term 'money' should not include credit. He quoted Ezra Pound, 'money is the measure of value,' but went on to explain that credit is the belief in money as the measure of value, when the money is not there to do the work, that is, without money, value is measured as if the money was there. Whether money and credit prove blessings or curses depends entirely upon the value they are made to measure.

It is not surprising that Heron never abandoned faith in the medieval doctrine of the Just Price, which was an attempt to take into account the good life of the producer, the good life of the consumer, and the wellbeing of the community as a whole. From the Christian point of view, money could only be tolerated as a measuring system in a society where some mechanism existed for working out 'just prices' for most of the commodities and services required in everyday life.

In a paper on *Money, Credit and the Creation* for the Christian Social Council, Heron considered St Augustine's precept that all human sin consists of the enjoyment of things which were meant for our use and the use of things which were meant for enjoyment. 'Is money a thing we ought to enjoy or is it something we ought to use?' asked Heron, and commented,

'Most of our difficulties in connection with our failure to understand money arise from the fact that we try to make it perform two separate and distinct functions. First of all, we ask money to measure values. Secondly, we ask it to give valid claims to them. This confusion of the measure and the claim is due to our inability to realise that possession and enjoyment are not necessarily synonymous. (Are they not even necessarily antagonistic?) That money can be used to measure values when it does not constitute a claim to them was shown during the war, when, although butter was 2/- per lb, the possession of a one pound note did not give its owner the right to buy 10 lbs of butter. The valid claim to the butter was the ration-card. The idea that merely because a man has plenty of money he should therefore be able to buy more than his share of a commodity which is in short supply is one that has always been repugnant to every decent human being.'

'Money is a civilized thing that must be used in a civilized way,' Heron told his audience on another occasion. 'If we insist on our money having absolute powers, then we run the risk of losing any benefit to be got.'

'Again a whole group of people may invest money in an industry, irrespective of whether the industry requires the capital or not, and if you have a big enough weight of money you can crash your way into any industry.'

A word which stank in his nostrils was usury. He considered that through the device of usury, people had been 'taken in on the ground floor' by the financial system. As holders of National Savings and Government Loans, and indirectly, through the investment of Insurance and Pensions Funds, interest is paid on money not subject by the lender to risk of loss by its expenditure in enterprises which may fail. If £100 is left to accumulate interest at 5 per cent yearly, the sum doubles itself in less than twenty years. This process has been condemned as immoral by the Greeks and Jews, the Christians and the Mohammedans. But it has survived all condemnation and is so entrenched in the social order that no one can release himself from its operations.

He told a private gathering of economists and businessmen in the early nineteen thirties:

'We blame the public institutions which are authorised to control the increase or decrease of the total of callable money available for private expenditure at any given time, but deflect our gaze from the doubling of our own million-fold 'small savings', with the resulting depreciation of the currency, which we express as rising prices. And we tend to overlook the "private bankers", Rothschilds, Morgans and a few others, whose immense operations on a world-wide scale ultimately determine how much above the total real cost of production shall be demanded in prices for the major constituents of our modern economy.'

Surveying the consequences of universal usury, Heron was driven back to the fundamental perception of C. H. Douglas that national resources are inherently the common property of the citizens in whose territory they are found, and that the employment of money to promote and utilize natural resources should be undertaken by the political government of each territory, freed from usurious swelling of the money units by accretions of interest, as though money itself were a commodity.

Heron preferred his information straight from the horse's mouth. He long remembered an evening in his Leeds home in the early 1920's. 'I got Major Douglas up to Hollin Lane and I asked my neighbour, the Professor of Mathematics, and I also asked Professor Smith, the Economics Professor, to come in and discuss it.' Between the Wars Heron was strongly taken with Douglas' analysis but never the uncritical enthusiast some of his friends were. He listened to other views and heeded other counsel. By 1941 he was distancing himself from the Social Creditors.

> 'They will miss the boat if they continue to sit back in their arm-chairs and imagine that good must result merely because the financial system they used to attack has now ceased to exist.'

Heron became a familiar figure in circles where the reform of the financial system was being discussed, especially those which accepted the relevance of moral considerations. Chief among these was the Christian Social Council, composed of representatives appointed by the Church of England and the Free Churches. As Chairman of its Economic Reconstruction Committee, Heron presided over a conference in 1935 which produced a pamphlet: *The Christian Approach to Economic Reconstruction*. This was followed a year later by *Monetary Policy: A Manifesto from a Christian Standpoint*. The document set out

> 'to seek for some new principles by which to regulate the influence of finance upon the peace and welfare of the different sections of the community to lay alongside those principles of business rectitude which have been operated by bankers hitherto.'

Its two main recommendations were that Government should actively foster stable price levels and check the movement of capital from one country to another for private gain to public detriment.

In June 1937 Heron was one of the leaders at a conference of Christian economists and businessmen chaired by the Archbishop of York, William Temple, and Professor H.G. Wood. This resulted in a report: *Monetary Steps Towards A Better Social Order*.

Heron was also an active member of the Economic Reform Club. In October 1937 he gave an address from the pulpit of Christ Church, Westminster, as part of a series arranged by the Economic Reform Club on the theme: 'What has gone wrong with money? It does not fulfil its function.' Heron's text was reproduced in the November issue of the periodical *Wealth*, under the title 'Money's True Function.'

Temple had previously involved Heron in a private enquiry into monetary policy. The Archbishop's influence enabled Heron to meet important Treasury and Bank of England officials. All these contacts led to his being co-opted onto an Inter-Party Parliamentary Monetary Commission. Its work was cut short by the outbreak of World War II, but not before Heron had the chance to meet Keynes.

All the above events ran parallel with, were interwoven with, Heron's very demanding full-time business career. They indicate the activity of his mind with regard to finance. It accompanied his daily business, it continued over his lunch-time beer at the pub, it even occupied much of the traditional Heron family weekend walks through the Hertfordshire lanes, which provided such ideal conditions for prolonged and profound conversations that his children accused him of not noticing the scenery at all. Heron himself ended a letter to the *New English Weekly* (July 1941) on 'Social Credit During War' with characteristic pragmatism: 'It is always the world we are living in, and not the one we are waiting for, which our financial theories must serve.'

Chandos

AT VARIOUS TIMES HERON SUPPORTED a great many movements and societies but the most cohesive influence on his intellectual life was provided by the Chandos Group, named after the Soho restaurant where it originally met to dine and to deliberate. Conviviality never disguised the high-minded purpose of members to pool their remarkable breadth of experience and erudition for the elucidation of a wide range of subjects of common interest. Their starting point for an evening's discussion would vary from world events of great moment to the publication of new developments in psychology or philosophy, from the solution of perennial economic chestnuts to specific problems bugging individual members. To continue discussions far beyond the patience of any restaurant, members adjourned to one of their homes. But the cross-fertilization of minds did not stop there. Started hares and undeveloped arguments were pursued in voluminous correspondence. Information had to be corroborated, evasive quotations secured and second thoughts circulated to keep the pot boiling until their next meeting.

Chandos had been started in 1926 among exponents of Major Douglas' Social Credit. The fortnightly informal meetings were later reduced to once a month. The original members were a strange Yugoslavian sage, Dmitri Mitrinovic, William Travers Symons (a marine insurance broker), Alan Porter (a poet) and two of Heron's friends, Reckitt and Mairet. A third, Demant, was added very soon. Heron himself could not join until after he left Cornwall in 1929.

For over forty years Chandos nurtured Heron's closest friendships. He who had missed out on a university education found himself at home in scholarly company that would have graced any Senior Common Room. It gave him first-hand insight into many new fields of expertise, not just through his fellow members but also through the distinguished guests it was the custom of the Group to entertain. The chief long-term significance of Chandos lay not so much in anything it achieved collectively, as in the aggregate of what it enabled its members to achieve individually. Nevertheless, it developed something approaching a corporate identity and philosophy as years went by. Reckitt, Demant and Heron, the last Chandos survivors, were still meeting in 1975, all in their eighties.

In 1932 Orage returned to England after a decade in France and America. Still intoxicated with Social Credit, he founded a new paper, *The New English Weekly*, a successor to the *New Age*. When he died suddenly in 1934 he was succeeded as editor by Philip Mairet, under whose editorship the paper fell into the hands of Chandos. One of the most celebrated contributors to the N.E.W. was T.S. Eliot. His association with the paper led him to attend Chandos and in due course he became a permanent member. He also joined the editorial board of the N.E.W. along with Jessie Orage (sole proprietor), Reckitt, Pamela Travers, Symons and Heron. Eliot was to make a particularly generous gesture underlining his attachment to the mission upon which the N.E.W. was engaged by selecting it for the publication of the last three of his *Four Quartets*, the first of which had appeared in his own *Criterion* shortly before it ceased publication.

Heron too contributed to the N.E.W., sometimes under his own name, sometimes under the pseudonym of Ealdorman or Aeldoman. His subjects included Inflation, Cartels, Lend-Lease and Leadership Management. One of them, *Prolegomena to the Methodology of the Study of Unnecessary Sweat* (February 1945) was printed as a pamphlet. In the N.E.W. Heron's thought was directly expressed. The contributions were short and had the merit of having been dashed off whilst the fever of the subject was pulsating within. Time for reflection and careful drafting tended to result in duller pieces of writing from Heron.

The produce of the Chandos vine was consumed in *The New English Weekly*, which called itself a 'review of public affairs, literature and the arts'. Its 'Notes of the Week', usually written by either Mairet or Reckitt after Chandos' deliberation, were full of interesting and provocative comment on current affairs. Much Chandos thinking was ahead of its time and thus unnoticed or disregarded. For example, Mairet and Heron insisted upon the right attitude to natural environment. Their view was simple. Human society depends upon the other kingdoms of nature both for its direct sustenance (food, clothing, shelter) and for the materials of whatever additional structures its civilization invents and becomes dependent upon. Society in turn reacts upon the natural environment. The sense of reciprocity and the right understanding of it were not only of immense and obvious importance in that material calamity attends upon neglect of them; their right cultivation was and is a condition of the psychic and spiritual health of a society and affects all its culture.

The significance of this aspect of the paper's influence has only recently been recognized. In an article in the *Agricultural History Review* (Vol 46 1998), Philip Conford claims that prior to the establishment of the Soil Association in 1946, 'the *New English Weekly* was the most important journal in the history of the organic husbandry movement.' He argues that besides devoting space to all the major figures in the movement:

'It was only in the pages of the *N.E.W.* that all these strands were brought together and worked into a coherent view of agriculture's nutritional, social and spiritual importance to national life.' And he concludes: 'When the full history of the movement's development comes to be written, the *N.E.W*'s role will demand a central place.'

It was Mairet and Heron who led the paper in developing its philosophy of husbandry. They were also pragmatic. Already in 1940 a reader was complaining of their 'manure complex.' From that time on, Heron kept a compost heap which, characteristically unabashed by modesty, he fed from his chamber pot. Other Chandos members had less conviction, being in the main townspeople with rural thoughts.

It was different with industry. Here Heron was supreme. He lost no opportunity for expounding his thesis that an increasing technical and functional emphasis in the daily work of society tended to divorce the worker from both his materials and the purpose of his work, for both were determined for him by overriding consider-ations of utility. Heron held that the industrial arts did not develop sufficiently from within, from the craftsman's own consciousness of his business. Hence the reduction of many or most workers to the position of replaceable parts of the productive machinery proceeded apace. What was the answer? A restoration of the responsibility of the worker for the quality of the work. This was an area of interest to which Heron had a practical contribution to share. Travers Symons led the thinking on finance; Mairet and T.S. Eliot had much to say on culture, and Maurice Reckitt had the reputation of being a 'Christian Sociologist.'

There was another development which had affected the Chandos Group, in no way planned or even perhaps expected. This was its evolution into a more and more explicitly Christian body. From the beginning, its members had recognized the place of religion as a cultural factor to be of prime significance, but there was no disposition to press this aspect of the matter in any doctrinal direction. This reservation was as completely accepted by its formally Christian members as by those who remained detached from any ecclesiastical conformities. It was never at any point explicitly set aside, nor did it need to be. But as time went on and new members joined, it became more and more evident that the cultural and socio-logical outlooks and judgments of the Group were being arrived at on the basis of what were clearly Christian doctrines of Man and Society. Such an evolution, if it could ever have come about at all, would have been worse than useless if it had been in any way the consequence of deliberate pressure. It is precisely the seed growing secretly which alone produces flowers and fruit. As with the seed, so with Chandos.

In his preface to *The Idea of a Christian Society*, T.S. Eliot wrote:

'To aim at originality would be an impertinence: at most, this essay can only be an original arrangement of ideas which did not belong to me before and which must become the property of whoever can use them. I owe a great deal to conversations with certain friends whose minds are engrossed by these and similar problems: to make specific acknowledgments might have the effect of imputing to these friends an in-convenient responsibility for my own faults of reasoning.'

The friends Eliot referred to included the Chandos group. Another of his books, *Notes Towards the Definition of Culture*, was dedicated to Philip Mairet.

The majority of Chandos members were involved with the Christendom Group, if only on the fringes, or as speakers at Summer Schools. Maurice Reckitt edited *Christendom: A Journal of Christian Sociology* and the editorial committee consisted of Reckitt, Ruth Kenyon, Demant and Widdrington. The Church Union Summer School of Sociology, usually meeting at an Oxford College, was in the hands of the Christendom Group. Heron was a regular attender and occasional speaker, sharing the 'bill' with distinguished names. He was also responsible for writing some of the syllabi and reading lists. Participants in the Schools were expected to prepare well, and his suggestions for reading were stretching.

Heron's participation as a speaker took place in later years. In 1941 he read a paper on *The Function of Industry in a Town*, the overall subject being The Future of the Urban Community.' He was responsible for reviewing and summarizing the discussions at the conclusion of the 1946 School on 'The Welfare State.' The 1954 School had as its theme 'The Technical Age: A Problem of Science, Humanism and Faith,' with Ritchie Calder describing the characteristics of the technical age, Leslie Paul dealing with the effect of technology on man and Heron left with the task of presenting a paper on 'Principles of Discrimination.'

Having prepared the syllabus for the 1957 School on 'Christian Living in an Expanding Economy', Heron was also given the job of summing up the School, following three controversial speakers – Lewis Mumford, Denys Munby (a critic of Christendom's economic thinking) and John Fitzsimons, a Roman Catholic priest formerly involved with the Young Christian Workers – Jocists.

At the Schools Heron thrashed out ideas with such people as Reinhold Niebuhr, Jacques Maritain, Nicholas Berdyaev, Julius Hecker, Christopher Dawson, Charles Williams, E. I. Watkin, and Denis Saurat.

What, if any, was the value of these Schools and Groups? Did they foster academic theorizing to little practical effect? How could Christians speak with authority on world government or industrial relations, nuclear testing or disarmament unless they had taken the trouble to study the basic technical factors involved?

The Summer Schools catered for those who were ready to take pains in this way. Some who attended each year were experts in one field or another: economists, scientists, social workers, industrialists. There were theologians and writers, and there were teachers, housewives, country parsons and students. The Schools had an effect on them. To those who attended, the discussions, with the common worship which provided a background and inspiration, presented a spiritual as well as an intellectual stimulus.

Heron got a great deal of stimulus from Chandos, *The New English Weekly* and from *Christendom*. He needed 'Galvanic Christianity', for he was that kind of person by temperament. The words of a French Roman Catholic were enough to galvanize him into action:

'Taken as a whole, our Christianity has become insipid. Despite so many grand endeavours to restore life and freshness to it, it is humdrum, listless, sclerotic. It is lapsing into formalism and routine. As we practise it, and as, in the first place, we think of it, it is a feeble, unavailing religion; a religion of ceremonies and observations, of ornaments and trivial solaces, with no depth of seriousness, no real hold upon human activities – sometimes with no sincerity either. A religion outside life, or one through which we ourselves touch with life.'

Heron had a continual battle with himself until late in years when prayer, poetry and spirituality coalesced. Meanwhile, he was continually enlarging his horizons and his influence.

Chapter Ten

A Working Hypothesis

AS KING ARTHUR'S KNIGHTS WERE POSSESSED by their quest for the Holy Grail, so was Heron possessed by a lifelong search for understanding of the nature of 'work' in all its facets. There was work and leisure, work and prayer, work and vocation, work and art, as well as work and freedom in industry, and of course, unemployment. Whatever he was vouchsafed to discover, Heron felt compelled to share in a stream of articles, letters, addresses and sermons. Consequently he needed several outlets. For many years he was well served by the 'Industrial Christian Fellowship', which provided a forum for both speaking and writing. When at the age of ninety-one he sought some copies of his pamphlets, the Honorary Librarian wrote: 'We do not think, in view of your personal involvement with the I.C.F. and your authorship, that we should invoice you, and hence the enclosed come with the I.C.F.'s compliments.' The 'enclosed' were, *Freedom and Control in Industry* (1943), *Christianity and Leisure in the Modern State* (1949), being his address from the pulpit of Southwark Cathedral, and *Will Automation Cause Unemployment?* (1957).

Prior to all these, a notable conference had been held in January 1941. It was the Malvern Conference. Its alternative title was the Archbishop of York's Conference – and the Archbishop of York was William Temple.

The holding of the conference was due to the courage of P.T.R. Kirk, Director of the Industrial Christian Fellowship. With his perspiration and Temple's inspiration, the success of the Conference seemed assured. Twenty bishops (eleven of them diocesan) with nine deans, parish priests, dons and laity, all gathered to hear speakers of the range and calibre of T.S. Eliot, Dorothy L. Sayers, J. Middleton Murry, V.A. Demant, Kenneth Ingram, W. G. Peck and Maurice Reckitt.

The conference was called in order to:

> 'consider from the Anglican point of view what are the fundamental facts which are directly relevant to the ordering of the new society, and how Christian thought can be shaped to play a leading part in the reconstruction.'

What impressed the British public was that here, in the middle of war, a great body of Anglican churchmen should put out a social message representing the mind of the younger and the older leaders, which, by its simplicity, its vigour and its brevity, made it plain that the social issue was a burning one for the Church of England and could never again be put in the background while men like Temple proclaimed it. In fact, the discussion during the conference was confused and chaotic at times and it seemed impossible that there could be any coherent or agreed report.

Drawing of his father by Patrick Heron in 1943.

But, as happened on many occasions, Temple worked through the night before the final morning session and prepared and presented his own draft – a breathtaking undertaking. It embraced all his own ideas and in a sense bore little relation to the speeches made. However, it was put to a grateful conference and adopted nem con. A few days later some members felt a little disquieted at the way in which the resolutions had been adopted, and there was a letter in *The Times* signed by, among others, T. S. Eliot and Alec Vidler, voicing their unease.

Nevertheless, nothing could detract from the remarkable event. One commentator referred to 'the diversity of thought represented there in doctrine, philosophical and political outlook – from a Conservative MP (W. Craven-Ellis) to Sir Richard Acland MP, from the evolutionary neo-Croceanism of the Dean of St Paul's (W.R. Matthews) to the Barthianism implicit in the utterances of some of the younger theologians.'

Heron attended the Malvern Conference and read a short paper on 'Vocation, Life and Work,' subsequently published in *The Guardian* (10 April 1941). He was particularly struck by Dorothy Sayers' lecture on 'The Church's Responsibility,' which was forceful, provocative and closely packed, but the meat was too strong for many stomachs. And she was particularly struck by some things Heron told her, as we shall see in a moment.

During the Conference, Heron gave Sayers a copy of a report, *What is Christian Education?* which was a piece of group thinking recorded by Marjorie Reeves and John Drewett. It arose out of the Christian Auxiliary Movement, which was a kind of senior members' attachment to the Student Christian Movement. Heron had become involved through his connection with the *Christian News Letter*. It was a part of the war-time effort to go on thinking positively and constructively.

Heron persuaded Sayers to write a 'Foreword' to the booklet. Her letter to Heron of 12 March 1941 is typically Sayers:

'I apologise very much for my delay in dealing with your Conference report. First of all the bag in which I was bringing it back from Malvern was stolen from me at Kings Cross. It was next heard of in a gent.'s convenience at Finsbury Park and after vegetating for some time in a Police Station, was returned to me, just as I was making up my mind to write and confess to you that it was lost for ever.

'By the way, in speaking at Brighton on the Archbishop's Ten Points – (point Nine – 'Daily work and vocation') I was able to get in an eloquent passage on the point you made to me at Malvern, namely that the worker was not allowed to make a really first-class product because it might spoil the market. The audience seemed rather impressed with this.'

The six page 'Foreword' was written, but that was not that. Sayers had asked Heron for more of his own writings on Work, and he sent her *Work, Leisure and the Creation* (Christendom, March 1936). She in turn shared this with her friend and collaborator, Miss Muriel St Clare Byrne, with whom she joint-edited a series called *Bridgeheads*. The series was opened with her own book, *The Mind of the*

Maker, and she referred to this in a letter and invitation to Heron of 20 March 1941:

'We feel that you would be the very person who would write us a short book ... on the lines of your article. My book, as you will see, is theoretical and deals chiefly with the work of the artist; and we are very anxious to get someone who can deal on the same lines with the work of the ordinary man in a machine age. I have touched on this subject in the postscript of my own book, but only, of course, very lightly. We feel that you are the person who has the actual practical experience, both from the management end and from the worker's end, of the difficulties and possibilities of a creative attitude to work in the factory. You would be able to give us the actual opinions and experience of employers and employed in a way that none of us literary blokes can attempt. What do you think of this suggestion?
'We attach very great importance to getting the practical side of our Series fully represented; but it is extremely difficult to find the people who possess both the actual experience and the will and the ability to express this in writing. If you like this idea, perhaps we might some day come and talk to you about it.'

Sayers admitted that she thought of Heron contributing to the Series as soon as she heard him speak at Malvern. Heron hesitated, for not only was he busying himself with the problem of clothing the nation in war-time, but he also realized his own difficulty in writing anything of book length. Sayers would not take 'no' for an answer and promised a collaborator if necessary. On 31 March 1941 she wrote to Heron:

'We are most particularly anxious to get a really sound book on this question of work and leisure and the paragraph in your article about 'the time allowed' and 'the time demanded' struck us very forcibly as being one of the most illuminating contributions we have seen offered to this particular problem. In addition, of course, there is that whole matter of the 'autonomy of technique', which needs to be got thoroughly into people's heads before they can deal with the relations between work and society. There is also, of course, the whole business of distinguishing between money and wealth, which is at the bottom of our financial dislocations. At present this always seems to be tackled either by financiers who know nothing and care less about society, or by idealists with strong opinions about society but very little experience of work. That is why we feel so strongly that you are in the position to give us a balanced view of all these matters.'

Heron agreed and they met at Welwyn to discuss it, after which Heron immediately put pen to paper. Sayers wrote to Heron on 6 May 1941 saying:

'It was marvellous to see you starting in on it like that straight away. I never had such a sensation of pulling down the switch and starting up the power-engine!'

By 21 May, Heron had written about 7,000 words which, as he told Sayers, he proposed to show to Mairet, Demant, Reckitt and Eliot, 'Just in case I have unwittingly tumbled into a heresy and partly because I want to direct their attention to a particular point.'

The title of the book was to be 'Work, Vocation and Ministry' and the seven planned chapters were to carry these headings: 1. 'What is work?' 2. 'The Rhythm of Work' 3. 'Vocation!' 4. 'Vocation and Machine' 5. 'Vocation and Finance' 6. 'Vocation and the Art of Government' 7. 'Where Theology comes in'.

The manuscript opened with a few pages, 'By way of Dedication.' Unfortunately only two full chapters apart from the 'Dedication' were written – 'What is Work?' and 'The Rhythm of Work.'

It was October 1941 before it was sent to Sayers and Heron wished there was more time to write but:

'My job here (Board of Trade) makes it impossible for me to do anything on Sunday except to recuperate. It makes me want to chuck this job and go off to Mirfield to write in peace. But I guess I'm preparing Chapter 5 (Vocation and Finance) for you here! It's a great observation post! Criticize. I don't know how to write yet. And use any ideas I toss up – any time – anyhow you like.'

Sayers was thrilled with what she read:

'I am so glad to see that you have started off with that extraordinarily moving story about the tramp. It contains our whole argument in an extraordinarily impressive way. I was speaking at a W. E. A. meeting the other night, and afterwards talked to some of the men there ... One little man, who had been all his life in the silk trade, seemed to feel quite passionately about letting the workers see the results of their labours. He spoke of the beautiful genuine silk this firm had made in the old days, and how the girls working on the looms never even set eyes on the fabric they were producing, and several of them spoke of the excellent results produced by allowing some of the munition workers to go over the ships for which they had been making armaments – and the pride with which the workers pointed out the sections of the work for which they had been responsible.'

(Sayers to Heron 17 October 1941)

'Is there *any* way by which Lord W can be bribed, blackmailed, or knuckledusted into giving you a fortnight's leave?'

'We will now try it on the publisher – only the poor man will be dreadfully tantalised by having this bit offered him and the rest withheld. Do move heaven and earth to get out for a bit. Faith and a long enough lever will shift anything.'

(Sayers to Heron 19 November 1941)

It is a tragedy that Heron never wrote any more of the book, although he continued to live its title. And the book has never been written by anyone else. Few people have grasped with penetrating insight what Heron knew. In one of his essays in *Theology and Society* (Easter 1947), Demant stressed a constant theme:

'The disease with which we have infected the world is that of the domination of life by economic values. This has all but destroyed our political freedom, debauched our culture and religion and stultified genuine economic activity itself ... The immediate problem ... for a recovery of political and economic freedom out of the matrix of the mass society is the separation of the economic system from the political. This can only be begun by recovering the proper purpose of economic activity. As Mr T. M. Heron, the only Christian businessman who has a Christian philosophy of business, as distinguished from the crowds who think they can Christianize motives inside a false frame, has said: 'The primary problem of planning is not "Education for leadership." but "Inquiry into the nature of the job." Recovery of economic and political freedom requires as the first step that each reverts to the nature of its own job.'

Heron wrote an essay in *Prospect for Christendom: Essays in Catholic Social Reconstruction* (Faber 1945) edited by Maurice Reckitt. Other essayists included: F. N. Davey, V. A. Demant, E. L. Mascall, T. S. Eliot, Philip Mairet, Henry Balmforth, Ruth Kenyon, Charles Smyth, Patrick McLaughlin, and W. G. Peck. The book was important but not entirely successful, for too many themes were covered in its 255 pages. The writers were 'Christendom' members and even that arch-critic of 'Christendom' thinking, Ronald Preston, had this to say about Heron's essay, 'Man at Work':

'Mr Heron has some wise things to say about the characteristics of the technologist and the machine tender, and writes well on absorption in work as analogous to absorption in prayer, since in both cases a man is giving himself to God.' (*Modern Churchman.*)

Heron's unusual but profound observations are worth stating in full:

'The Christian doctrine of work which alone can make for Peace and Plenty on this planet must be one which starts with man as "a creature" created by God, for a purpose we but dimly know and know only as we worship. For the Christian, "Work is the proper exercise of the creature." Its objectives must be linked with our vision of an end in beatitude. Its method must be the method of prayer. Its challenge is to each one of us as an individual person to use the particular talents with which we have been endowed – our only real property – on the raw material which has been placed in our way. This statement is of course merely a restatement of our traditional belief. And it is only of academic interest until it is related to the problems and conditions which surround us to-day. Can a financier or a machine-tender really pray at his work to-day? Can he practise the presence of God as he plans his next deal or struggles against the monotony of his nut-tightening? Can he see in the thing he is making or causing to be made something which is being made for Christ's sake? Let us admit without reservation that unless in each case the Christian can answer these questions with a simple affirmative, he must, if he is logical, give up either his Christianity or his activity in relation to money or the machine.

'Full acceptance of the doctrine that work is prayer leads in fact to the conclusion that many of our present industrial activities should be classed, as lending money at usury and the gladiator's occupation were once classed, as callings which no Christian can pursue – he should indeed be excommunicated if he insists on doing so. But before we indulge in industrial heresy-hunts, it is important that we should be quite sure that we really know what our doctrine means.

'The mystic tells us that the spoken prayer leads the mind to a silence in which the self loses itself in the wonder of God's glory. The mind goes with the words and the body severs its connection with the mind before prayer is experienced in the highest form known to man. After the silence, verbal prayer bridges the gap and leads the mind back to consciousness again. But the essential part of prayer is its central silence. It is this which gives value to what precedes and what follows it.

'Much the same structure in the technique of everyday work has been discovered by many men of whom it might truly be said that their prayer was in their work. First, the mental preparation before the body is launched upon its labours – the conception of the job. For the Christian this involves the selection of an objective, the conscious reasoning about it in relation to his understanding of God's purpose, and the request that His blessing shall accompany the body into its labours. The non-Christian's conception is, of course, the product of his passions and his philosophy. After the conception comes the process or task of carrying it out, and this always involves some struggle with intransigent raw material and some arrangement and re-ordering of a part of the natural world to suit the purpose in hand. And here something very significant is known to happen, for it is a matter of common experience that the labourer sometimes loses himself in his work and that when he does so, his load is eased. There is a strong resemblance between this condition of the body absorbed in what we call work and its state in the silence we call prayer; and the reason for the resemblance is that in both cases man is giving himself to God – in the one instance to God at work in the natural creation, in the other to God at rest in the spirit. Whether the worker is a Christian or not, whether the work itself is of a highly specialized nature like that of the lumberjack, does not appear to affect either the essential quality or the frequency of these experiences of the silence in work. The man who emerges from his preoccupation with the making of a chair may find his body relaxed and his soul refreshed in much the same way that the mother is eased in body and lifted up in spirit when her child is born. Certainly these 'happenings' occur most frequently in what we call the artist's work, but in every activity essential to man's well-being we can always find some people who insist upon working as artists. It is upon this discovery of what takes place in the natural world that the Christian doctrine of work has been built. To the question: 'Can a man pray as he works with money and machinery?' the clear answer is that, from the purely practical point of view, neither money nor machinery can ever be used aright unless man does in fact pray as he works with them. The very structure of the physical universe not only invites him to pray as he works, it also frustrates his work if he does not.'

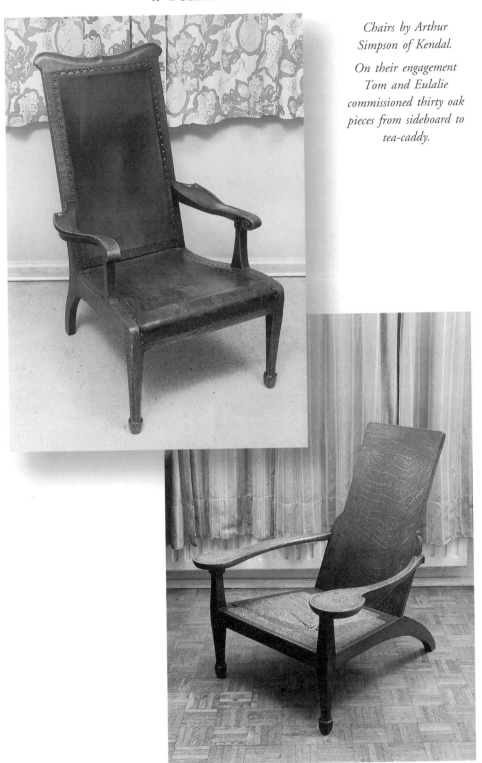

Chairs by Arthur Simpson of Kendal.

On their engagement Tom and Eulalie commissioned thirty oak pieces from sideboard to tea-caddy.

Before publication, Heron had sent his essay to Eliot, Demant, Mairet and Reckitt for comment. Eliot replied:

'I admire this paper and am in particular impressed by the account of the relation of prayer and work and the "silences." This seems to me to hold good for writing poetry, so it ought to be good for making chairs. (A great deal of the verse I see might have been made in High Wycombe.)'

Chapter Eleven

Dreaming

I. The Christian Frontier

HERON WAS A DREAMER. A dreamer is unafraid. He is not frightened of being told that he has his head in the clouds. He will not wilt at criticism and he is likely to brush obstacles aside as he tries to dream his dreams true. Few dreams will materialize into reality but he goes on dreaming.

Retirement in 1953 left Heron free to dream. He did most of his dreaming in the small groups to which he belonged and in which he was not always the only dreamer, although often he was. An interesting group was the Christian Frontier Council. It was a fellowship of thirty or forty lay men and women who held responsible positions in secular life and who met regularly from 1943 onwards to explore with each other the practical implications of their faith. Although the Council was a lay initiative, it was formed with the deliberate assent of the leaders of the Church of England and the Free Churches. Its founder was the missionary J. H. Oldham, doyen of the ecumenical movement and editor of the *Christian News Letter*, which he had started in 1939. Though insufficiently forceful to keep the ecumenical movement out of the hands of the ecclesiastical institutionalizers, Oldham was quietly influential in all kinds of ways. He, with others, had been influenced by the writings of Baron von Hugel and Jacques Maritain. Von Hugel held that the relation of Church to Society is a dual one. Oldham wrote:

'In its confession of faith it makes universal claims. But in its institutional embodiment it exists within society as one human interest or activity alongside of other interests and activities such as government administration, law, industry, education, medicine, science and art. These other spheres or departments of life, von Hugel maintained, have a proper autonomy of their own – not an autonomy in respect of God, but an independence of any ecclesiastical direction or control.'

('The Frontier Idea', *Frontier*, Winter 1960)

Heron's relationship with the Christian Frontier, which lasted for over twenty years, was a marriage of strong minds, held together by mutual respect, characterized by fruitful stimulation rather than by conformity. Like a larger, looser-knit Chandos, it introduced Heron to people with a wide variety of public experience and responsibility, men of the calibre of John Maud, Kenneth Grubb, George Goyder, Peter Kirk and Walter Moberly, and of women such as Laetitia Fairfield, Marjorie Reeves and Monica Wingate. As with Chandos, meetings led to correspondence and friendships developed. The Frontier proved a gold mine which Heron exploited to great effect when seeking speakers for Sherrardswood School speech days.

The minutes of the C.F.C. meetings show that Heron's frequent individual contributions to discussion often bore a blend of originality and profundity, but tended to lack the scholarly moderation of his colleagues. He also presented some papers of more careful argument as basis for general consideration. In one analysing the metaphor of the 'Frontier', we find the typical Heron remark: 'There are no perfect marriages on earth and none at all in heaven, yet the marriage bond is a good example of a Christian frontier.' And in another entitled 'Sabbath Observances in an Atomic Age' he wrote:

'I think we should be very chary of legislating about any form of Sabbath Day Observances. As I see it, the Sabbath will very largely take care of itself if we can get a right attitude to our work', and 'Today we simply do not know what guidance the Church ought to be giving to workers engaged in many of the most significant activities of our time. In consequence we have a bad conscience about it if we are to have a Christian Sunday.'

For many years the mouthpiece of the Christian Frontier Council was Oldham's *Christian News Letter*, latterly edited by Kathleen Bliss. This was to be incorporated into the quarterly *Frontier* edited by John Lawrence. Contributions from Heron appeared at times in both journals.

At one Frontier luncheon at the time of the Korean War Oldham reviewed the world situation and said: 'let the soldier get on with his work and the armament worker with his, but at the same time let us all rebel against the present feeling of impotence and work creatively to avoid the unparalleled destruction which threatened to wipe out so many things that God loves.'

Heron was challenged by this suggestion to the point of feeling that it was directed at his own lassitude in thinking compartmentally about the world. Frontiers were there to be crossed. Was he in danger of being attacked by the bug of complacency, whose first sting brings disorder to the mind so that all problems appear too big or complex for 'me' to tackle? Not for long. It re-stirred in him a sense of foreboding about the deification of the specialist and the expert. Heron wanted the larger view and wider vision in which specialization is subordinated to a comprehensive view of human affairs. Heron knew what happened to ancient civilizations which fell under the burden of over-specialization.

Nevertheless, Heron considered that a contemporary failure rested in the universities. There was too little cross-fertilization between disciplines. Modern universities failed to provide that constant intercourse between the Faculties which alone could serve to merit or justify the title of 'University.' So Heron unfolded his dreams to a number of his friends:

'Does anyone imagine, for example, that Oxford, Cambridge, Yale or Harvard could call a halt to their present preoccupation with the turning out of graduates and settle down to a decade's task of reconciling the findings of one branch of learning with those of another? Yet that more than anything else is what is needed today. Theologians, philosophers, historians, mathematicians and physicists, working together to re-educate themselves, might possibly change the whole direction of our learning.'

How would this be done? Not by establishing another 'university' with its segregated faculties and departments. Heron, ever audacious, wanted a 'true' university set apart 'for the purpose of seeing that at least some specialists in each branch of learning are acquainted with the laws and values which others have discovered in theirs.' And let it be in Vienna or Constantinople.

Who should be involved in such an enterprise? Heron produced a list of fifty-four names to indicate the range and quality of people he had in mind, from Fred Hoyle to C. S. Lewis, from Michael Polyani to Barbara Ward. Only some were already household names but almost all had sallied forth from their ivory towers to reach a wider public. To ensure that enough feet were on the ground, Heron included many with administrative experience but the links with the civil service and politics were strictly limited. It is noticeable that although the scheme was the dream of a man of industry and commerce, there was no suggestion of including his own kind. Was there a lingering hint of personal diffidence in academic company?

Heron shared his vision with a number of people including Dorothy Sayers, who responded on 29th November 1954: 'I fear I have no practical ideas to offer about a new university.' She then outlined what she saw as the chief characteristics of the medieval university: the poverty and discomfort of the students, their high spirits and violence, and the magnetic quality and reputation of the Masters who attracted them. Her last point was: 'that every addition to the syllabus should be adopted in the teeth of ecclesiastical opposition, and under peril of the Inquisition. (For 'ecclesiastical' read 'scientific' and we might get somewhere with this part of the programme). Well, I am always ready to hear of some new thing.'

Heron replied on 1 December 1954.

'Your list of medieval requirements is admirable. But we are living in a scientific age! What is required is that expensive but austere accommodation should be provided in some secluded place near Constantinople or Vienna where you and I could spend six months of the year together with about 100 other interesting people drawn from both sides of the Iron Curtain. What we should do is a matter we can discuss when I see you! The main thing is to get contacts quite free from the political and economic stresses which are beggaring the position to-day.'

And Heron was serious but not single-minded enough to pursue his idea. So his 'true' university remained a dream.

Undeterred and undaunted, he had another plan which came before the Christian Frontier Council in 1955. This time it was for an 'Institute of Christian Sociology.' This brought him into conflict on fundamentals with many of his Frontier friends. Oldham's view had always been that being a Christian does not give a person special insights in the decision of questions that call for technical knowledge or for painfully won wisdom in dealing with practical affairs. For Oldham, being a Christian was to have a certain attitude to life and to cherish certain values. Oldham had a low doctrine of the Church. He did much to delay the birth of the British Council of Churches.

Heron, though no institutionalist, was a churchman and for him being a Christian changed one's perspective about everything else. It was a total way of looking at life and living it out.

Sociology was the arena of conflict in this instance. The word sociology, first used by Comte, was a philosophy of society, conceived in the scientific enthusiasm of the nineteenth century. When sociology lost its philosophic soul, it gained a whole world of new knowledge and of practical influence. Economists, political scientists, demographers and social statisticians, public opinion investigators, pathologists, psychologists and public health specialists of every description became indispensable components of the machinery of government and national administration. The determining factor, to all appearances, was the urgency of each great national Power not to be out-distanced in the race for scientific and technical supremacy (with a secondary emphasis upon general physical welfare) but it was highly questionable whether human beings were willing or able to be conditioned to the service of such an overruling objective, incompatible as it was, to Heron's mind, with the nature and divinely-appointed destiny of man. Christians who thought like Heron could not accept such an elevation of means into ends, believing, as they did, that there is a destiny of man, revealed by God in Christ, which is in accordance with the perfection of man's nature as a created being. Demant, with whom Heron shared his idea of an Institute of Christian Sociology, wrote, 'The good life is in the Christian faith something to be recovered rather than created by man ... Man's true nature is bought back with a price.' Philip Mairet, who read Heron's draft paper, comments on Demant's words:

'Implicit in that belief there is a scale of values, an inherent criterion for the valuation of any aims that societies may set before them; and such a criterion of values is the unifying principle, which alone could re-philosophize Sociology, or almost theologize it.'

Accordingly Heron could assert:

'The faith of the Christian Sociologist is that an authentic Christian Sociology could change the order in which new scientific, technical and social knowledge is brought into the world; for the direction, balance and proportion of every new human enquiry are affected by the nature of the enquiry which preceded it. Searching always for signs of the 'civitas dei' in the 'civitas mundi', the Christian investigator may hope to discern social trends and possibilities whose existence is hidden from minds occupied solely by the search for power trends.'

Before the Christian Frontier Council met to consider Heron's proposal for an

Institute, a report of the Social and Industrial Council of the Church Assembly on 'Moral Re-armament' appeared. Heron used this 'timid, formal and scrupulous' report as a basis for a forceful article in the *Christian News Letter* (April 1955), where he was able to introduce the subject of Christian Sociology and the need for an adequately staffed Institute:

> '. . . if the separate specialist skills of this age are to be used in a way and for an end of which theology can approve. Such an institution, though staffed by dedicated Christians, should resolutely leave all evangelistic work to the Church: research, teaching and exhortation are separate functions of civilized man. And it is only as each is accorded due respect in its own sphere that our vision of their ultimate fusion in worship can mediate for us.
>
> 'A Christian sociology would not be Christian unless it started from Christian conceptions of man and of society; neither would it be sociological unless its findings could be applied and tested in the practical world of affairs, where Christians must co-operate with non-Christians in making political and economic decisions.'

In a surprising editorial note in the same issue of *Christian News Letter*, John Lawrence distanced himself almost out of sight from Heron's proposal. Perhaps his editor's conscience felt trapped. Disliking both options, either publishing Heron's article (which he disagreed with) or turning it down, he did in effect do both. It was a mischievous editorial, for it was seeking to damn a proposal that had not yet been considered by the Council. Moreover, Lawrence had ensured that he had the majority of the Council on his side. According to Lawrence and his cohorts, everything about the proposal was wrong – its name, its method, its timing, its academic respectability. But he gave himself away in the last sentence of the editorial. 'Christians from the Catholic tradition sometimes put forward a "Christian Sociology" which makes Christians from the Reformed tradition inclined to dispute whether any sociology is Christian in the proper sense.' It was the Christendom connection which frightened Lawrence.

Heron, properly incensed by the editorial, wrote a spirited defence of his proposal; but Lawrence rejected this further article. Heron sent his article to members of the Christian Frontier Council and of the Social and Industrial Committee of the Church Assembly and to about one hundred other people who were thought to be interested in the project. He asked them to say:

1) Whether they think that the case for the use of the term 'Christian Sociology' has been substantiated?

2) Whether they can suggest an alternative title which, whilst safeguarding the position of those who believe that there is a tradition of Christian doctrine about Society, will at the same time permit the co-operation of those whose approach to social problems has been more individualistic and ethical?

Heron sent his paper to this large number of people because he was convinced:

'that the chances of bringing a worthwhile Institute into being will be prejudiced if a fairly large number of people who have come to believe in what they call a Christian Sociology have this title turned down without being given the opportunity to state their case. Many of us are sick and tired of the contemptuous dismissal of our claims by what I may perhaps be permitted to call the 'London School of Economics' type of mind without any attempt being made either to understand what we are saying or to answer us rationally.'

(Letter, Heron to John Lawrence 23 June 1955).

The case against the name (and object) of an 'Institute of Christian Sociology' was this. Sociology is a science, in regard to the nature, status and scope of which there is the widest diversity of opinion. It includes or involves an illimitable range of theoretical problems of endlessly different kinds, and an incalculable number of concrete, practical questions most of which require quite distinct approaches and methods of treatment. To suppose (so the argument went) that one could bring them under the cover of one single Institute, let alone of the small edifice limited resources would allow to be erected, seemed to be a basic misunderstanding of the world and of the real nature of its problems. Moreover, the adjective 'Christian' was mistrusted in this context. And here the fundamental division of view surfaces which proved irreconcilable then and persists to the present day.

Heron saw things differently from the majority of his fellow Frontier Council friends. For him there had always been Christian Sociology, changing in its modes and forms of action with the successive phases of secular culture. According to this view, Christian social thinking never actually takes the form of an ideal alternative to the existing pattern of society. The function of Christian Sociology is to conserve the values that are primordial and essential, and to facilitate their rehabilitation in the new forms of society.

For this to be done, in the spirit of wisdom, by Christians gifted and specialized for social understanding, is a problem redefined on a larger scale than ever by the secular mobilization of the social sciences. It was the greatest challenge that Christian Sociology had had to encounter since the rise of Capitalism.

Christian Sociology does not oppose the pursuit of the social sciences; it aims to regulate them, much as St Thomas Aquinas said that true virtue did not eliminate but regulated the nature of passions.

When the Christian Frontier Council met on 12 October 1955, they had before them Heron's paper and that of Professor Michael Fogarty on 'What an Institute of Christian Sociology Might Be.' The discussion was long and argumentative; but there was little support for Heron's proposal, except from John Wren Lewis of I.C.I. Heron's own advocacy on this occasion was not good.

It was not the end of the matter. Heron pursued his idea through another organization to which he belonged, St Anne's House, where he was assured of a measure of agreement.

The episode illustrates some of the virtues of the Christian Frontier Council; the breadth of its exploration, the fearless debating of the issues thrown up and the abiding respect which survived even such fierce disagreement as Heron's proposal provoked. Even twenty years later there is an unmistakable warmth of friendship in the occasional correspondence between Lawrence and Heron.

The failure of one dream never deterred Heron from pursuing another. No-one aware of the realities of nuclear rivalry during the so-called 'Cold War' could fail to agonize over the problems and dangers involved. To pacifists such as Mairet and Heron, the matter called for special soul-searching and re-assessment, yet it was difficult to acquire enough technical and practical knowledge to join in the debate with confidence.

In 1957 Mairet wrote to Heron with characteristic open-mindedness, commending Denis Healey for a speech in the House of Commons directing attention to the possibility of keeping the use of nuclear weapons within limits. Heron's attitude was also typical. He could not leave it entirely to others, but mere re-assertion of old principles was too simple to be fair to those carrying the burden of responsible office. He had to know more. In a letter to *The Times* (February, 1976) he recalled:

'As a member of the Christian Frontier Council I played a small part in the formation of the Institute of Strategic Studies, and until I resigned because there was a waiting list of applicants for membership, I attended all its sessions.'

The Institute of Strategic Studies, in the formation and operation of which Rear-Admiral Buzzard played a leading rôle, attempted to reconcile military strategy with the moral concerns of a variety of churchmen in evolving an acceptable approach to warfare in the nuclear age. Writing of the I. S. S. long after its demise, a fellow member of the C.F.C., Professor George Wedell, has said:

'The notion that there was an intellectual case for non-nuclear response to possible Soviet aggression was a relief to those among whom I think Tom Heron was pre-eminent, who could not conscientiously support unilateral disarmament and therefore had to find a third way which would permit the West to defend itself by means other than a total nuclear response.'

It was one of the stranger experiences of Heron's life to find himself a party to confidential military information and working alongside distinguished brass hats with a common purpose.

Sometimes life and dreams were not so different.

II. St Anne's House

ST ANNE'S HOUSE TOOK ITS NAME FROM THE CHURCH OF ST ANNE, Soho, destroyed by heavy bombing in 1940. In its old parish house, which was still standing in 1943, the then Bishop of London, Geoffrey Fisher, opened a 'Centre for Christian Discourse'. It was to be a place in central London, easily accessible from Whitehall, Westminster, Fleet Street and Bloomsbury, to which legislators, civil servants, journalists, writers, publishers and broadcasters etc. could come in order to review the rapid and radical changes in social structures and in ideas and sensibilities in the light of Christian social thinking and action. The House thus attracted a very wide public, which included artists of all kinds, doctors, social workers and psychotherapists, scientists and scholars in widely different fields, politicians, industrialists and civil servants. Many of them were Christians seeking a better understanding of Christianity or of contemporary problems; but the majority were non-Christians, either seeking to understand Christianity better, or, more often, attracted by the concern with, and insight into, contemporary problems displayed in the House's programmes. Lectures were given by a very wide range of experts, some of them men of great distinction, others young and working on original theses of importance. Many other more selected groups of 12 to 15 people met at the House for more intensive study, often composed of people never previously involved in 'Christian Discourse'.

The arrangements under which the House was enabled to carry out these activities were something of an inspired improvization. The Director and his assistants received their stipends by duplicating this work with parochial duties in the area, using for worship the old Tenison Chapel, erected in 1700 as a preaching house and later known as the Church of St Thomas, Regent Street (alas, now demolished), with St Anne and St Peter, Soho. The House as such had no regular revenue, only that which it received as donations or from the small fees charged for admission to lectures. Until 1956, the St Anne's Society and the House of St Anne, Soho, were one.

The first Director was Patrick McLaughlin, a man of astonishing versatility and remarkable gifts. Heron liked this man, even if at times he found him exasperating. Maurice Reckitt had known Patrick McLaughlin for a much longer period and later wrote, privately, of his former friend – for there was a breach when McLaughlin resigned his Anglican Orders to 'go over to Rome':

'He had what is conveniently described as a chequered career, during which his remarkable gifts had never brought him the recognition that he might have earned and should have enjoyed. There are certain things to be remembered about Patrick which may help to account for this. Patrick, as his name might suggest, comes of Irish stock, and he has a good deal both of the natural charm and – it must be added – the 'blarney' often exhibited by that race. Again, he might have been an actor and would almost certainly have been a pretty good one; he has a beautiful speaking voice and sense of 'theatre' that might have taken him far. There is a third characteristic which may not have been so generally noticed. Patrick is by nature a Mediterranean Man, and it is surely no accident that he has finished up (for the present) in Rome. I have never heard anyone with a power to sum up a complicated debate as he could. I have met very few people who had read as widely as he has, and had so much power of 'recall' from that reading. It is tragic that he has never been able to produce a first-rate book; with his resources he should have written half a dozen.'

When Heron first met him, McLaughlin was a country vicar in Essex and much concerned with the Christendom Movement. But his great achievement, and this at the time when Heron knew him best, was building up St Anne's House into the most intelligent Christian Forum in London and keeping it going for a dozen years, from a discouraging start in World War II. There were crises galore and nearly always money problems. Heron was not alone in dipping into his pocket – and often – to help McLaughlin out of a 'temporary' difficulty. The Mediterranean connection, mentioned by Reckitt, was always there. Heron was as likely to receive a letter from McLaughlin written from the home of, say, la Contessa Rayneri (to whom he introduced Heron) in Bordighera, as from a Benedictine Monastery in Florence or Rome. The hospitality was grand in each case.

St Anne's House provided Heron with an emotional and aesthetic outlet and the tragedy is that it was never allowed to fulfil its potential. The narrow vision of the Church authorities could not perceive the value of such a place. On the surface it appeared to be a place for making intelligent and educated people aware of the full implications of the Christian Faith in the contemporary world. There was nothing novel in that. Where St Anne's was different from anything else that was available was that it challenged and stimulated the whole man. The ideas of such people as Dorothy Sayers, Patrick McLaughlin and Heron were that the activities would touch the whole person. There was the Forum, appealing to the discursive intellect, where discussions were conducted at the highest level. The most authoritative secular specialists met the most intelligent and 'aware' kind of Christian commentator and apologist. This meant drama – with such plays as *Waiting for Godot, Mother Courage* and *The Strong are Lonely.* Discussions on literature must include contemporary writers: Camus, C. P. Snow, Graham Greene, C. S. Lewis, Kingsley Amis, Colin Wilson and a wide range of poets. For the visual arts current trends in painting and pictorial symbolism should be studied. All types of music should be embraced and understood.

Then there was 'Ecclesia' – the appeal to the spiritual man, that is, that which believes, loves and worships. Experiments in suitable forms of liturgy should take place. Lectures and instructions should be part of the regular programme. Dorothy Sayers noted something which Heron underlined:

'It has been represented to us that there is a public (chiefly professional) which is anxious to be informed:
a) factually – What the teaching of the Church actually is on this or that point of faith or morals;
b) historically – How such doctrines came to be formulated, and how the Church has coped in the past with the perennial human problems.'

In short, lectures in 'hard doctrine' were required which were quite definitely instructive and not 'explanatory.'

Patrick McLaughlin thought very highly of Heron, and remembered him with these words:

'Tom shared our vision to its outermost periphery and was active in organization as well. Tom was not only a dreamer, though he was one: he was primarily an ARTIST, a man who saw beyond external shapes to interior planes and structures (like Cezanne), a man who could both visualise and fabricate new fabrics in new colours and then create and manage an industry to manufacture and to sell them. Every Heron is a pioneer, well named after a bird with exceptional beauty, with legs long enough to see distant horizons and wings strong enough to carry him there.'

Heron was on the Advisory Council of St Anne's House, which was one of the most imaginative ventures of its time and kind. Many names engaged in this venture are those which have already been mentioned, showing the amount of cross-fertilization that took place. The Bishop of London was President, whilst the Vice Presidents included Nevill Coghill, T.S. Eliot, D.M. Mackinnon, Sir Charles Peake and Lady Rhys Williams. The Chairman of the Council was Dorothy Sayers. The House remained active till 1957, when it was closed by the Diocese of London owing to lack of resources and Patrick McLaughlin went to Rome (literally and metaphorically). Some of those who wished its activities to continue formed the St Anne's Society, which met whenever space could be found. The St Anne's Society continued its work until 1977. During these years it was directed by the Rev. Gerard Irvine from St Cuthbert's, Philbeach Gardens in Earl's Court. The character of the continuing venture is well indicated by the list of its Council members: James Mark, Assistant Secretary, HM Treasury; A.B. Saunders, Principal, Ministry of Works; John Addey, Assistant to Commercial Director, Peter Spence & Son Ltd; Tyrell Burgess of *The Times Educational Supplement*; John Davison, Head of the Industrial Management Department, Brooklands Technical College; Michael Fogarty, Professor of Industrial Relations in the University of Wales; P. Racine Fricker, Composer; T.S. Gregory, Producer in the Third Programme, BBC; John Heath-Stubbs, Professor of English Language and Literature in the University of Alexandria and poet; Mary Hesse, Lecturer in the History and Philosophy of Science, University College, London; R.W. Ladborough, Fellow of Magdalene College, Cambridge; Peter Parker, Director of Booker's Engineering Holdings Ltd; Maurice Reckitt; Lady Rhys Williams, Chairman of the Cwmbran Development Corporation; James Seth-Smith, Actor and dramatist; E.A.O.G. Wedell, Principal, Ministry of Education; John Wren Lewis, Deputy Research Controller, ICI; and Heron.

Dorothy Sayers had caught the spirit of the original St Anne's House in a speech she made on St Anne's Day in 1957, the year of her death.

'St Anne's House was founded as a centre of liaison between the Christian faith at its most intelligent level and the secular intellect at that point where it is most conscious of social and ethical responsibilities. It is precisely at this level that the problem of communication becomes most acute ... especially in view of the very rapid development in social and industrial techniques which is changing the aspect of the world about us ... The men who handle these new powers are not without conscience. They sincerely desire to know what they ought to do ... But they cannot understand the

Christian language or accept its premises; it is for us to learn their language, and to undertake that most difficult of all intellectual disciplines, which is to start imaginatively from their premises without for one moment allowing the will to assent to the imagination.'

Heron was happier in the St Anne's milieu than in many other groups. Although he enjoyed the Christian Frontier Council, some of its members were serious in a different way. He liked Oldham, who was friendly, gentle and sagacious in addition to being excessively serious. Oldham was radically Protestant, more Lutheran than Calvinist, with an inapprehension of wit and, a fortiori, of irony. Oldham disliked Maurice Reckitt, whom he regarded as not merely misguided but positively frivolous and dilettante. Oldham could better stomach Heron and Philip Mairet.

St Anne's House was different. It was like bursting into a room full of light and dancing spirits. Heron could introduce his friends Herbert Read and Bernard Leach into this atmosphere. Through all kinds of interconnecting activities Heron was meeting an ever-increasing number of people. Some of them were encouraging him to explore new territories.

Chapter Twelve

New Pastures and Lasting Relationships

H ERON'S CURIOSITY CONTINUED WITHOUT CEASING until his dying day. Nevertheless some eyebrows were raised by the news that in his seventies he was conducting a 'Science Group' at his home, for truth to tell, science had been singularly absent from conversation in the Heron household. It soon became clear that this was no flash-in-the-pan pensioner pastime, rather a serious extension of his lifelong attempt to understand God's Creation.

Heron's belated pursuit of science stood normal education on its head. He began, typically, with the icing on the cake, the major recent advances and their philosophical implications. Only later, sometimes, did he master basic ingredients. Some would say he was a little gullible where science was concerned. Perhaps naive is nearer the mark.

The origins of what might more properly have been called a 'Religion and Science Group' illustrate the integration of Heron's life, the way old strands formed new threads. Remembering meeting Lord Northbourne long before, Heron wrote:

> 'His mind was playing on many of the points which my Science Group had wrestled with during the last twenty years since the St Anne's course on 'Religion and Science' inspired us to start a group here.'

Its hey-day began with an influx of fresh members in January 1961, when their number included research chemists from nearby I. C. I. Plastics, physicists, a doctor, a scientific librarian and an individual pharmacist as well as non-scientists. At their first meeting they drew up the following list of subjects for discussion: the similarity of the processes of scientific discovery and religious development; the nature and reality of scientific statements; the nature of proof and the limitations of scientific method; the difficulty of communication – the breakdown of the visual symbol in science into mathematics, and in religion into mystical statement; the holistic aspect of religion; the necessity to judge religion and science at their best, not to confuse the issue by pseudo-science nor to base discussion on what outsiders think that the Church is saying.

The recollections of one member, Philip Marriott, are worth quoting at length:

> 'The more outrageous suggestions came from Tom. Provocation and Socratic method, complete with a delightful innocence, was usually his method of attack, quite often with a twinkle in his eye. He introduced Teilhard de Chardin to us by easy stages. We followed him to Church and his archaeological work in the Gobi desert, and learnt of his early life and problems with the Church. Always a scientist, but always

reconciling his work with the purpose of God and creation. We read his later work with continued interest but I am sure with some difficulty ... But Teilhard de Chardin provided us with great questions and we understood some of his answers. *The Phenomenon of Man* is not easy to follow but with proddings and queries from Tom we followed from the priest to the scientist in the light of daily life. I do not think that we became neo-humanists, as de Chardin would term it, but perhaps we gained a glimpse of his exposition of divinity. So we came together in that long room in Heron's home, beautiful and spacious, standing and looking south over the area ... listening to the throaty chuckle, the extraordinary questions, the notions of perverted biology, and sipped our tea or cider interspersed with commonsense interjections from Eulalie his wife to bring us back to this everyday reality:

> Either you had no purpose,
> Or the purpose is beyond the end you figured
> And is altered in fulfilment.

'Whether we became better Christians or worse agnostics as a result, is hard to say. Certainly we derived much enjoyment and good fellowship and a glimpse of other minds in our thinking aloud. And Tom would think this a worthy aim and a happy result.'

It was Philip Mairet who had introduced Heron to the thinking of Teilhard de Chardin, the palaeontologist and French Roman Catholic Jesuit priest, whose writings were proscribed during his lifetime but who gained posthumous fame. Mairet was concerned with the official translation of Teilhard – no easy task in view of the extraordinarily difficult language used. Teilhard's genius was to reflect on diverse elements of nature, from electrons to nations, to root them in the behaviour of the original matter of the universe and to synthesise them in a single Idea: the concept of a world converging on itself. Each person has a stake in the future and must use his wits to preserve Life and improve its quality.

Heron swallowed Teilhard whole. He eschewed any critical appraisal. Teilhard appeared to be saying what Heron wanted to hear, namely, the interrelation of all things. In an article inspired by Teilhard, Heron acknowledged

'There are no completely isolated spheres of life ... (a fact) recognised by both saint and scientist, though the scientist knows that he has to isolate, as it were, a particular phenomenon in order to study it, and the saint knows that he must first regard his free will as if it were his own, in order that he may surrender it.' ('Towards the Redemption of Science', *Anglican Theological Review*, January 1961. A shorter version appeared as 'God and the Spontaneous', in *Frontier*, Winter 1960.)

It is significant that the years in which Heron was most preoccupied with science were also those in which he became preoccupied with writing serious poetry. The new field of exploration and the new form of expression interacted. The language of each enriched the other. Perhaps the uncertainty of his grasp of science made the resort to metaphor inevitable.

Shortly before his seventy-seventh birthday, the combination of poetry with the dialogue between science and religion introduced Heron to yet one more of those circles of pioneering kindred spirits with which his whole life was peppered – in both senses! This was a group calling itself the 'Epiphany Philosophers' based in Cambridge. It had been in existence since 1952. In Heron's words:

'For fourteen years they have been slowly working at the idea of becoming a group of Christian contemplatives whose secular job was scientific research, and in particular studying the theory of communication and information.'

Prominent in the group were Dorothy Emmet, Fellow Emeritus of Lucy Cavendish College, Cambridge and sometime Professor of Philosophy in the University of Manchester; Margaret Masterman, Director of the Cambridge Language Institute; and R. B. Braithwaite, a former Knightsbridge Professor of Moral Philosophy of Cambridge.

In 1966 the Epiphany Philosophers started a substantial journal, *Theoria to Theory*. In its way it was an influential avant-garde periodical. Esoteric? Yes! Pretentious? No! *Theoria to Theory* was about the cross-communication of ideas or it was nothing. For years Heron had been trying to eradicate the divisions between religion, science, technology, art and other spheres of thought and action. In reviewing the first issue of *Theoria to Theory* in the *Cambridge Review* (21st January 1967), Bernard Towers made the point that the Epiphany Philosophers were asking 'monastics to renew their vision, for scientists to stop trying to be fashionable, and be curious instead'. This was the flavour of one issue. Another looked at 'A World of Spirits?'; 'Theism as a Scientific Hypothesis', and 'Behaviour under Stress in Mountaineering'. Another discussed 'Myth; Tuning the Human Instrument', and commentated on Schumacher, and 'Philosophy and Traditional Culture'.

Heron saw the first number and immediately became an enthusiastic supporter. He submitted one of his latest poems, as Eulalie duly reported: 'Tom got a lovely letter from Dorothy Emmet. They want his poem (Peacock Science) for *Theoria* and want to meet him.' The second number duly carried Heron's poem.

Peacock Science

Knowledge is just a point of view
its form dependent on a chosen stance
and on the training mind and eye receive.
Two eyes can see that something is behind
the object single eye perceives.

Science is single-eyed and splintering,
one hundred Argus eyes
for ever taking photograph of fact,

hoping to find in fact
infinity.

Some day
these hundred eyes will decorate a peacock's tail
and guard the gate of Paradise.

By this time – January 1967 – Heron was becoming thoroughly involved. On meeting the group, he discovered they were in crisis and 'in urgent danger of being turned out of their H. Q.', as he wrote to his son Giles. 'I have started the ball rolling with Frontier and we shall try to raise £40,000.'
By way of suggesting a donation, he went on:

'To give you an insight into their methods, we all dressed up in long white vestments with albs for mattins, evensong and communion, and used the Anglican prayer book – you couldn't tell which were priests and which were men and women – they believe in equality.'

As so often, an important part of Heron's contribution was practical, organizational. He plunged into such matters as fund-raising, negotiating for property and planning the establishment of an institute to extend and perpetuate the work of the group in the United States as well as in England. He helped it to find suitable people for specific roles. As a result, Geoffrey and Gladys Keable moved to Cambridge so that Geoffrey could act as Chaplain. Similarly Eric Southall, a close family friend since the First World War and retired senior accountant with Price Waterhouse, moved to Cambridge and gave the benefit of his experience.

Heron himself helped in other ways. Professor Emmet has a vivid memory of an occasion on which the group met in a windmill in Norfolk. They used to go there for a week at a time for mutual enlightenment, the gathering being both conference and retreat:

'At one meeting Tom and Jack (Eulalie) and Philip Mairet all came. When they arrived they were all behaving like old and tired people. There was something of a crisis over getting out a number of *Theoria to Theory*, (not an unusual event!), and this roused all Tom and Mairet's editorial flair. They joined in and helped edit it. This had such an invigorating effect on them that by the end of the week they were bathing in the sea, going for fair-sized walks, and eating large-sized meals.'

Eulalie described these meals as 'indoor picnics.'

'No serviettes, – eating everything off one plate. It was a free-for-all, people too busy talking to notice who needed the butter or cheese, so you all reach out and help yourself. Clothes – well – almost beatnik standards.'

Heron endeavoured to interest religious communities in the thinking of the Epiphany Philosophers, with more eagerness than success. In his appeal he pleaded for members of religious communities to collaborate with the philosophers and scientists who were struggling towards some sort of belief in the idea that contemplation, like the intellect, was a tool which man must learn to use properly if his work is to prosper:

'Moreover, prayer, contemplation and ritual are now seen to have played an important part in holding past societies together. In short, the scientist is inviting the mature Religious to dialogue at a deep level.'

In reality this was an invitation to an esoteric few. George Every, a Kelham Father, was already associated with the Epiphany Philosophers. One or two other Religious expressed interest, but the majority failed to respond – perhaps less because they did not care than because they did not understand.

Heron's connection with the Epiphany Philosophers was concentrated rather than prolonged. As early as December 1969 Eulalie confided in Gladys Keable:

'I'm beginning to think that Tom has shot his bolt as far as T to T are concerned – I mean as far as active participation is concerned. I'm sorry, for the T to T was an immense stimulus to him for two years or more and he got a great kick out of being useful to them.'

By April 1971 that change had come to pass. 'I have no regrets that we're disentangled from that set-up though I wish them well.' Even so, correspondence continued and Margaret Masterman or Ted Bastin in particular called in at Welwyn as late as 1976. Sharing the community life and worship, however, became history.

As for most octogenarians, life began to contract for Heron. The lion's share of his time and energy began to be consumed by concern for his contemporary friends and relations. More and more of those who had played important rôles in his life had left the stage.

One of the first to go had been Albert Mansbridge, the great educationist and founder of the Workers Education Association, who died in 1952. Heron's friendship with, and admiration for, Mansbridge dated from his Leeds days, when his contribution to the W. E. A. there included a talk explaining how a board of directors appointed by the workers could run a factory properly. Heron kept in touch with Mansbridge on and off ever after but their association became closest when the Mansbridges came to live in Welwyn Garden City. It became a Heron family ritual for Mansbridge to come and read aloud from 'The Hunting of the Snark' on Christmas Eve in his quavering growl of a voice. He was someone Heron felt he could turn to for advice in a crisis, as he did on the outbreak of war in 1939.

Heron had already lost another of the men he most greatly respected with the tragically premature death of Archbishop William Temple. It was through Mansbridge's W. E. A. in the early 1920s that Heron had first encountered Temple, then Bishop of Manchester. Their paths didn't often cross but Temple, with his left-wing sympathies, appreciated Heron's writing and speeches on economic matters and called on his talents from time to time. It so happened that Heron was the Temples' guest at Canterbury in September 1944 to address a weekend conference. Heron curtailed his visit as Mrs Temple was anxious about her husband's gout, but Temple died very soon afterwards.

Two of the Herons' dear friends for some forty years were Pedro and Pilar Penzol. Pedro, who was Professor of Spanish Studies at Leeds University for more than twenty years, proved a great asset to The Arts Club. Cultivated and amazingly erudite in all the arts, he was a 'natural' for Heron in the cause of modern painting, having been a fellow student and friend of the celebrated cubist painter Juan Gris. He strongly endorsed the Herons' estimation of the artistic talent of their young son Patrick and for years provided valuable encouragement even after he retired to his native land. He died there in 1965.

Much nearer home, and more difficult to adjust to, was the death of T. S. Eliot the same year. The importance to Heron of his friendship with Eliot is incalculable for it operated at a deep level in both men. Indirectly it became important to other members of the family too. From their first meeting Heron recognized in Eliot something missed by many of Eliot's admirers and critics alike, namely his warmth and richness. Recognizing these qualities enabled Heron to remove some of the drapes surrounding Eliot and so their friendship was genuine. The 'Dear Eliot... Yours Ever, Heron' of their early correspondence became 'Dear Tom... Yours Ever, Tom,' Each entertained a deep respect for the other's integrity and originality of thought. They also felt able to relax into banter. In a letter of December 1954 Eliot wrote:

'I enclose quite irrelevantly, a small contribution of my own as a Christmas card for you and your family. I suggest it can be adapted for the mantlepiece by folding inside out with the verses to the wall.'

Heron's reply included the confession:

'Human nature being what it is, the card is going on the mantlepiece folded so as to show the superscription.'

The loss of such a friend hit Heron even harder than perhaps he might have expected. 'Ever since I heard of Tom's death I have been feeling a strange loneliness as if part of my consciousness had been taken away from me.' For solace he and Eulalie together turned again to the legacy of Eliot's writing. Eulalie's letters are illuminating as usual:

'We are very much wrapped up in Eliot these days – we keep reading him aloud – parts of the Four Quartets – the brilliant early poems which I am not so well acquainted with and just now the *Notes on ... Culture.*'

She added a characteristic reflection:

'It is the case with few people that you can get to know them better after their death than you did in life. But it is true of him.'

A friend of whom that could never have been said was Leonard Gray, who had worked long and closely with Heron as Chairman of Cresta. He was a big man in every sense of the word, a Scot of great charm and generosity, of wide interests and abilities, and modest withal. One of the foremost pioneers and pillars of Welwyn Garden City in its early days, he had built No. 76 Brockswood Lane for himself and his family. When they were fledged, wishing it to continue nourishing rich family life, he let it to the Herons at well below market rent for over twenty years. He also left his Bluthner baby grand in the large drawing room so that his tradition of musical soirées could continue, attending when he could and contributing Hebridean songs in his fine, high tenor voice. He was in Montreal when he heard that at last the Herons were to leave for a much smaller house. He wrote with imaginative feeling:

'Thanks for your lovely letters about the house. It is of course your house rather than mine because you have had all that time to express your personalities on it, and it has certainly appreciated the loving care you gave it at all times.'

Geographical separation had made contacts increasingly rare but Gray's death in 1969 was another sad loss. It left no consolation equivalent to Eliot's poetry.

Philip Mairet made an early appearance in these pages and the friendship, begun in 1918, lasted until the death of Mairet in 1975. The day before he died, Mairet received the sacrament of anointing and started a letter to Heron. It was the last time he put pen to paper:

'I am having an extreme time. What the French call the last phase of life's flickering – l'Agonie. I am un agonisant. I don't pray for the end, because I think that w'd be wrong. But I cannot but look forward to it now & then. Well, it is an universal human experience.
What a human being ...'

and there the letter ends.

The two men were both different and similar. Mentally boisterous and reckless (Heron), against the quieter and philosophically reflective (Mairet). Yet Mairet was mentally agile and his reach in ideas was greater than Heron's. Mairet was an Anglican in 'praxis' and a Catholic European in aspiration. Heron was a Church of England Anglican. Mairet was always a wordsmith, occasionally inspired, and was more fervent, fulsome and fluent on paper than Heron could ever hope to be. If he did not enter the enclave of the 'very best' in the spheres of thought and action in which he worked, it was because he had a quirky, philosophical mind. He was no match for Heron's 'downrightness' and verbal gifts. As commentators on human affairs, the two men were erratically far-sighted, though usually in-sighted. On social concerns, Heron was crisper than Mairet. Above all, and more important than all their words and despite Heron's occasionally bombastic manner and authoritarian pronouncements, they were humble men trying to live out their Christian faith, praying their prayers, wrestling with their consciences and seeking God's will for their lives.

John Peart-Binns recalls seeing an old, frail, slightly shabby figure, serving a weekday Mass for Bishop Ambrose Reeves, who was then Mairet's parish priest at St Michael's, Lewes. The conspicuous man of letters and the anonymous servant at the altar were one.

Heron's estimate of Mairet was contained in *The Times* obituary notice, which he wrote:

'He came of a family of distinguished watchmakers, a true European, whose exceptionally wide ranging mind led him to pursue many activities and to take part in movements which, in their time, were regarded as "avant garde."

'In his early years he joined the Arts and Crafts Movement in Chipping Campden, where he specialized in designs for stained glass; in particular, he designed, for Sir Gilbert Scott, a window in the Anglican Cathedral of Liverpool and in Sussex a window in the Downland village church of St Pancras, Lewes.

He was associated with C. R. Ashbee and Sir Patrick Geddes; his book, *A Pioneer of Sociology*, was published by J. M. Dent in 1936. He was active among the early Fabians. Soon after the First World War, Mairet joined the Old Vic Company, with Lilian Baylis, acting under the stage name of Henry Cohen when Robert Atkins was Director.

From the stage Mairet turned to journalism, first with Orage, then editor of *The New Age*. When he died, Philip took over as editor of the *New English Weekly* (which Orage had founded two and a half years before) and continued to edit it until 1949. Essentially a communicator rather than an original author, Mairet used this journal as a channel, or perhaps more accurately a mirror, through which many talented thinkers found a means of expression.

During this period Mairet became closely associated with T.S. Eliot and, through his influence, joined the Church of England. This brought him into contact with, and action for, the Christian Social Movement, especially with the Christendom Group, of which his great friend, Maurice Reckitt, was chairman. He was a keen ecumenist as were other leaders of that group and was a frequent contributor to its journal, *Christendom*.

Internationally, Mairet became intensely interested in Adlerian psychology. He translated several of Adler's books and wrote a memoir, *An ABC of Adlerian Psychology* (Kegan Paul, 1926). His brilliance as a translator is evident in his translation of Emmanuel Mounier's *Personalisme* (Routledge and Kegan Paul, 1952). He shared the personalist outlook of the famous editor of *Esprit*.'

Mairet's humble estimate of his own worth was expressed in a letter to Heron on hearing that Eliot and Heron were trying to enlist a Civil List Pension for him:

'Publicly considered, what is there to show? Certainly not my harmless but undistinguished services as a craftsman in stained glass etc ... or the four years interlude as a Shakespearean actor of mediocre talent. My fifteen years editing the *New English Weekly*? Well, as a bit of public service, this ranks, I should say, with the pastorate of a non-conformist church of the same length – and who would expect the Minister in his old age to get an extra pension for that? My services to the Frontier Council? The only thing that did them any good was my organizing the group of psychiatric doctors and producing, with them, a book that brought the Council a profit of 2 or 3 hundred pounds: but it's not really much of a book. My own books? *A Treatise on The Nature of Aristocracy*, 1930, which almost nobody read and which I now strongly disagree with much of; and two biographies, written more out of piety than inspiration, nothing to boast of anyway. Articles and reviews galore, of course, but not as much of that as hundreds of other equally obscure persons have produced. No, if I were the Treasury Secretary concerned with such a proposal as this, I should turn it down – flat.'

(18 November 1961)

Eliot and Heron were a formidably persuasive pair in their appeal to the Prime Minister's Appointments Secretary. They were successful on Mairet's behalf and in 1962, the year before the Pension was granted, a small grant was made to Mairet from confidential funds at the disposal of the Prime Minister.

Heron caught the evocative harmony between himself and Mairet in 1974 in a poem entitled simply:

For P. M.

I wake in philosophic mood
and, copying my Maker, say
I am.
And there is nothing else at all!

Then slow into my presence comes
an ordered train of subjects who
just wait upon my sovereign word,
and instantly I am becomes
the Royal We.

We are the trees outside my window pane,
my watch, the Bible by my bed,
my wife, my kith and kin,
my many friends alive and dead,
my morning cup of tea brought with *The Times*
and that strange line of Eliot's
that last night sent me back to Blake
and I must tackle now I'm wide awake.

How friendship interpenetrates!
Opposing minds unite as one
and only part to cleave amain
when there is something to be done.

Absence refines communication
when we is one.

The correspondence flowing between Mairet and Heron was large in volume, often provoking response and counter-response in quick succession. They threw into the mill of their dialogue their latest gleanings from any and every field of human endeavour. They pulled no punches for their goal was understanding; agreement was incidental. Sometimes they would include others in a correspondence chain. Reckitt and Demant were regulars in this.

The death of Geoffrey Barlow in 1976 ended another of Heron's long friendships, one based on the mutual respect and affection developed through nearly half a century of association in business. Well into his eighties, Heron could be seen, interrupting his poetry writing to pore over the trade returns of Allied Shoe Repairs' more than four hundred shops. Heron kept this last toe-hold in business by way of repaying Barlow in kind for the twenty years he had contributed as a Director of Cresta Silks. Eulalie's first cousin, and nephew of her 'Uncle Jim' who was Cresta's first Chairman, Geoffrey had helped Heron in the exploratory negotiations that led to the establishment of the firm. Since those days, Heron had had ample reason to agree with *The Times'* obituary description of Barlow as 'a man of outstanding kindness and generosity who did good by stealth.' In fact a brilliantly successful yet gentle tycoon.

One of the few contemporaries to outlive Heron, Lewis Mumford (1895 to 1990), was another friend and correspondent. Mumford knew Heron on and off from 1938 onwards. They met in Welwyn Garden City during one of Mumford's visits to F.J. Osborn. Mumford was drawn into the Chandos Group by Heron and was stimulated by the people he met there. For Heron it was another unexpected and fruitful relationship. Mumford belongs in the prophetic sphere. World-renowned for his books on civilization, he has been dubbed a sociologist, but preferred to be called a generalist. Although regarded and respected as an academic, he had no degrees of any kind. Two of his most influential books are *Technics and Civilization* (1934) and *The City in History* (1961). Sharp with his intellect and pungent with his pen, he had an independent mind. He was never politically committed, although he engaged in political activity, noticeably over the banning of nuclear weapons, but his pre-war writing was fiercely anti-capitalist and hostile to the idea of competition. In 1958 Mumford was saying: 'As a young man I was attracted by Socialism, now I am both conservative and radical' – a description of Heron too? Mumford did not share Heron's Christianity, so in their verbal and literary arguments on such matters as an atomic civilization, the nature of statesmanship, or automation, Mumford made Heron re-examine his postulates.

In some ways you only find the flavour of Heron's life in his family setting. A good look at the four children does not take you far beyond the range of their parents' interests: Patrick, with his artistic and critical gifts; Michael, now Dom Benedict, with his deep and wide spirituality; Joanna, with her generosity, natural hospitality and concern for the coming generation; and Giles, with his feeling for the earth, its conservation and fruitfulness, and his willingness to give a helping hand to the young who are floundering.

The continuing vitality of Heron's example and philosophy of personal vocation, the development of each person's unique gifts for a greater purpose, is manifest in the service and achievements of his six grandchildren. Their careers demonstrate an individual's ability to get things done harnessing social conscience, artistic talent and articulacy in writing. Besides achieving much in a variety of the arts, from architecture to mosaics, from personal jewelry to enhancing public buildings, they have between them created a city farm in London's East-end, sharpened linguistic precision through close-range reporting on the Kremlin, pioneered and promoted community architecture and action planning, created one of Ireland's leading conservation organizations and carried the struggle for freedom of information into the citadel of the United Nations.

Heron liked a saying of Sir Thomas More: 'Nothing can be wise that is not practical and I teach my children philosophy to fit them for living in the world, not above it.' He tried to heed Thomas More's advice. Heron was stronger on philosophy than on certain practical matters, particularly those which had to do with domesticity. He was not a handyman. His large and capable-looking hands were not given to nimble work such as replacing a fuse. The kitchen was a foreign country to him. He didn't often make a pot of tea. He was no gardener. He said he could not remember the names of any wild flower apart from the dandelion and the daisy.

The paramount influence in the home was Eulalie, always Eulalie. Without her pervading presence and sweetness of temperament, masking a sharp intelligence and penetrating depth, Tom Heron would never have found fulfilment in his work and in his other interests. She allowed him to be free-willed and still-centred. Without her, it is likely that he would at some point have gone off the rails, not easily finding his way back. This does not mean the marriage was free from turbulence because one partner subjugated herself to the fiery darts and erratic whims of the other. Eulalie's strength was rock-sure, Tom's much less so. He was a bit larger than life, a bit Falstaffian. Eulalie could not and did not try to be everything that Tom needed. In 1915 he was writing to her: '. . . I am not wanting the impossible. I am wanting the divine and you have got it in you . . .'

Like many women, Eulalie sacrificed a great deal for her husband, children and their happiness. She was not in the least interested in being the wife of a high-class Bond Street dress firm's managing director. But in the end, as at the beginning, though not always in between, Eulalie was the divine instrument which held course through fine and foul weather alike. On her eightieth birthday (3 December 1971) Heron could write:

> You have not changed. Your eyes still sparkle when
> a new found friend or cause wins your commitment,

> whilst I go juggling on and on and on
> trying to add another billiard ball
> to those I barely keep in circulation.

Two of Eulalie's sisters spent their last years in Welwyn Garden City. One in particular had a part in Heron's life.

Leila Mary (1893–1973) was a rare and brilliant person. She won an open scholarship to Somerville, took Hons. Mods. and then English. Her working life was almost entirely spent as a lecturer in training colleges, mostly in London. After she retired and had various small accidents, it was agreed that the best thing was for her to get a small house in Welwyn to be near the Herons. She hoped to find some literary work to do, coaching and teaching. But nothing permanent was offered and as she did not have much domestic ability, and even less inclination, her days were empty. Her last years were tragic.

Yet Leila's mind never stopped working, and as there was nothing on which to bite, to get her teeth into, she became frustrated. London had given her a rich life – concerts, theatre, meetings, above all students, students with young lives, adventurous spirits and energetic minds. Leila had combined extraordinary mental virility with physical vitality, external energy with inner glow. Heron wrote a poem, 'The Rocket Bursts', after she died in March 1973. It ended:

> With jet propulsion you out-ranged the skies,
> and now at rest in orbit send to Earth
> new data about creativity.
> Love yields its secrets to integrity:
> poetry our only pure articulation
> lights the long road to New Jerusalem.
> Flare forward, Leila!

Heron was strongly attracted to Leila. There were periods when his sight was dazzled by her and these led to anxious troughs in his marriage. But whatever else Leila and Heron shared, it was not any prospect of family life; rather a meeting of minds and a firing of imagination. If Leila had something of Emily Brontë, Dorothy Sayers and Marghanita Laski in her, it was probably her own limitations, not theirs, that kept her spinster. Perhaps she suffered a little more from her heritage than did her other sisters – from her brilliant, awkward Congregational father. She had a deep distaste, almost a phobia, where childbirth was concerned. Much better than the animal world was the mental world, which she found noble, exciting, almost divine. She was able to convey her inner vitality and consuming critical enthusiasm for all that interested her in her teaching and in her writing. Some of her occasional articles and reviews in such periodicals as *The New English Weekly* seem today as fresh and as illuminating as when they appeared. She saw all Heron's poems. Some did not survive her comments: others were the better for them. Leila was something of a Mary to Eulalie's Martha. Later in life Heron was wise enough to see that in Eulalie he had in fact both Martha and Mary and the source of his happiness.

Another of Eulalie's sisters, Kathleen, read science at Newnham and then moved to London and gained a doctor's degree in medicine. She never practised. Instead, she married Joseph Dalby, a priest, ten years her senior, who had been partner in much of the idealism and adventure of Heron's Bradford days. Having inherited a good deal of money from his father, he retired early and bought a house in Surrey with a beautiful and enormous garden. Generous hospitality was always extended to the wider family and many of their friends, particularly to Philip Mairet. Joseph attended Chandos. After Joseph's death, Kathleen remained in the house for a little time before moving to Welwyn. It was hoped that the three sisters would help each other enjoy their late years. It was not to be. Leila died in 1973 and Kathleen suffered a stroke.

When the time came for Tom and Eulalie to leave Welwyn, in 1978, they were fortunate in going to live with their married daughter Joanna, who lived in a wonderful setting at Selside near Kendal, on the edge of the Lake District. It is a place of beauty and wildness. Nature is allowed to reign and spreads its seasons comfortably across the calendar year. It was the perfect place for Tom and Eulalie to spend their final years. The degree of comfort and contentment they enjoyed as they lived out their later eighties and early nineties was a tribute to the extreme generosity of Joanna and Bernard, whose own family life had to be radically re-shaped. Their sacrifice became only too evident with Bernard's sudden tragic death in 1982, leaving Joanna to carry her self-imposed burden alone, a prolonged act of vocation in the mould of Heron's own personal philosophy and example. His mobility diminished, but not until the very end did his mental agility. Lines written by him on his ninetieth birthday include these words:

Another day.

I look out on the world
And my heart leaps
As something tells me
I am part of it.

I look inside myself
And find in art and liturgy
The silences that speak the Word
When time has passed away.

I see in autumn colourings
The world of all things new
That man made in God's image
Was created to enjoy.

I hear ancestral voices say

To labour is to pray
And know the Word will work in me
From now till Judgement Day
Or if there is no Judgement Day
Throughout eternity.

3rd January 1980.

Chapter Thirteen

The Great Day

HERON ALWAYS WANTED TO ARTICULATE HIS VISIONS IN WORDS. That is how they were conceived, if only through a glass darkly. He was often wishing he could write a book as so many of his friends did but his one attempt, on *The Doctrine of Work*, was never finished.

One can only conjecture why so articulate a man with so much to say should fail in that ambition through thirty years of retirement. Despite his prodigious self-confidence, his curtailed scholastic training left him with an impatience with, and distaste for, methodical scholarship and a soupçon of inferiority in the literary company he kept. Perhaps he no longer wanted to write a book that represented the heart of all his struggles to improve society for God's sake. His later years concentrated instead on recognizing what God was constantly doing for man. The abandonment of Cresta's idealism by his successors contributed much to some such change.

If not a book, perhaps a collection of articles? Heron approached T. S. Eliot in 1954 to see if Faber and Faber might be interested in publishing some lectures. Mairet and Demant encouraged him to publish a paper he had given at the Church Union Summer School of Sociology in 1954. Eliot liked the Summer School address and wondered if the compressed lecture, 'if carefully planted, tended and watered' might 'grow into a book by itself. The stuff is so good that I should be sorry not to see it preserved.' Eliot realised that Heron was having difficulty attempting to write at book length. He gave some advice from his own experience:

'I might, I hope, without presumption, offer one hint from my own experience. When one has got into the habit of writing at a certain length – and a good deal of what you have written has been for public delivery, that is to say of a length to take not more than an hour or so – then it is like attempting to exercise new muscles, to write at a different length. My prose stretch, so to speak, was formed early in life by writing leaders for *The Times Literary Supplement* and a leader in those days had to be just about 3,000 words. For a long time after that I found that whatever I had to say turned out to be 3,000 words. If it was less, I padded it out, if it was more, I boiled it down – all this quite instinctively. At a later stage a good deal of what I had to write was for platform delivery – that is to say about 5,000 words and I gradually found it possible to talk about a subject at that length. The problem of making a prose book a complete whole is something I don't think I have ever quite mastered. I suspect that I still work, thinking in terms of single essays, and then doing a certain amount of unravelling and knitting to put them together. This, at any rate, is my view in retrospect of my experience up to an age somewhat more advanced than your own, and my desire is to encourage you to contemplate a book making all the use possible of the 'snippets and articles' which you say you have by you.'

Such a book, however, never materialized. His writing took a different tack.

Heron's life had always bubbled with humour. It could erupt at any moment. Probably this aspect of his character has not yet emerged clearly enough, for humour is notoriously difficult to define or describe. He saw the funny side of the serious and, conversely, he valued the importance of humour. For him it was a vital function of human life, the Divine Comedy. It expressed itself in a lifetime habit of composing comic rhymes and jingles on any and every sort of event, be it of purely domestic relevance or of national importance.

> Hey diddle diddle
> can't rank as an idyll
> but give a poor doggie his bone.
> My spirit does tingle
> When I make a jingle
> and why should it tingle alone?

Heron was a sort of self-appointed poet-laureate or court jester. For example, Eulalie's confusion at the introduction of decimal currency provoked the following:

Decimal Day

> Sing a tuppence-ha'penny song
> Granny bought Ryvita
> told the man her change was wrong
> was he trying to cheat her?
> Would not let him have his say
> Said it wasn't funny
> What a most unpleasant way
> to welcome nice new money.

Entertainment was usually the prime mover as is evident with

> Fee fi, fo, fum
> I smell a red chrysanthemum.
> When you are dead you shall be tossed
> to decompose and be compost.

Often however they betray genuine underlying opinions, as when he entitled some verses 'Women's Glib'. At the very least they record topics interesting him at the time.

On the occasion of their wedding anniversary in 1930, Heron wrote a sonnet for Eulalie. It was called 'Renewal'. The uniqueness of his writing a poem devoid of humour marked the solemnity with which both of them regarded the challenge of their new life in Welwyn Garden City. Largely in blank verse, this poem was conventional in theme, poetic diction and imagery. It could fairly be described as an exercise 'after' Shakespeare. It probably had no successor during the following thirty years. None has survived.

A muse, like the wind, bloweth where it listeth. It seems that Heron's muse found 76 Brockswood Lane uncongenial. Perhaps that beautiful house on the edge of the woods had too strong an aura of its own. Eulalie was finding it too large and agreed with the muse. Whatever the explanation, after moving down the road in 1961 to number thirty-eight – half the number and half the size! – Heron the poet suddenly broke into song.

It may be that the onset of poetic creativity was related not only to the new home but also to his passing the landmark of three-score-years-and-ten, which can affect the optimistic as well as the superstitious.

Nothing clearly foretold the remarkable burst of poetic creativity of Heron's seventies and eighties, when he wrote no fewer than one hundred and twenty distinct and distinctive poems. Writing them became the dominant activity of the culminating twenty years of his long life, bringing many new friendships besides enriching the old.

In these years his working hours centred more and more on a chain of thoughts, visions, mere glimpses even, all of which had recognizably religious dimensions. Though he continued to pay close attention to what was happening all over the world, those events ceased to be as much the chief substance of his concern as its occasion. As the object of his searching gaze shifted, so did the appropriate form of expression by which he could describe what he found, from prose to poetry.

Although Heron was still capable of writing flippant verses, his main inspirational motivation was now deeply serious. He set out to do something that can never be easy – to interpret the eternal truths of the faith by which he was inspired to enlighten not only his own personal problems but the particular contingencies, potentialities and dilemmas of the age.

In a letter of September 1962, Heron replied to Leila's comments on one from the first startling batch of poems:

'I'm not surprised at your saying you haven't yet got the full meaning. Neither have I. But some time before, I had arrived at the conclusion that poetry was the language of prayer used for inter-human communication.'

This remark provides a key to understanding both Heron's individual poems and his poetic achievement as a whole. Many readers find they need such a key.

Like prayers, many of these poems were dialogues, in name as well as content. Like prayers, they are the utterance of a personal voice, often speaking in the first person. And like prayers, they responded to incidents of daily life from the hail stripping his cherry blossom to astronauts landing on the moon. Through his poems, Heron sought to penetrate beneath the surface of the tangible and visible in search of meaning and guidance. They approached eternal mysteries such as the problems of good and evil, of pain and suffering, of innocence and original sin, of free will and obedience.

This prayer-like characteristic was reinforced by the language he borrowed from the Bible and from Anglican liturgy. For example:

> I only know
> I is the end
> ordained for Me.

or again, writing of a seed:

> Faith tells me it will germinate
> according to its kind.

The same goes for his imagery, and herein lies one of the difficulties for many readers. They may not share his religious culture – forget the question of belief – and so the significance of Heron's short-hand references escapes them. While 'Eden' and 'Jonah' for example, are common currency, 'the Kingdom' and 'the Tree' are less so and mention of Patmos, Baal and Omega begins to be exclusive.

The vocabulary presents a few hazards of its own, like rocks beneath the innocent surface of his colloquialisms: nescience, for example, or Homunculus. Heron had no intention of sparing his readers the dictionary where he himself found so much delight. These difficulties are superficial, however. They even have their advantages. Non-Christian readers come to these poems fresh and unblinkered. Many such have found them illuminating, inviting and even inspiring. One wrote: 'I liked your poems so much. They gave one so great a sense of worthwhileness.'
The fundamental sense in which the poems are difficult lies in the struggle waged in them between intellect and mystery. In some cases the message is oracular.

> 'The obliqueness and 'toughness' of the utterance, in contrast to the simplicity of the vocabulary, intriguingly places the meaning of the poem just beyond the grasp of immediate comprehension.'

This was one of the perceptive comments made by Neil Gill, one of Heron's Garden City circle of friends, in a critique he wrote of *Call It A Day*, the only published collection of Heron's poems. When it appeared in 1977, 'cerebral' was the term he preferred. 'The style is one that calls primarily on the reader to use qualities of intellect in responding to the poems.' Gill cited Heron's penchant for puns, paradoxes and recondite allusions.

Another friend to whom Heron sent some of his draft poems was Herbert Read, who since the Leeds Arts Club days had earned a great reputation as a poet, a critic, a writer on art and a pioneer of the modern movement He appreciated Heron more than Heron's poems. He wrote in a letter dated May 1968:

> 'Your poems remind me of those now written, late in life, by I. A. Richards. They are interesting as apophthegms, gnomic utterances, but they do not conform to my

definition of poetry – they are not essentially musical. But they can be polished into real gems.'

Gnomic utterances! Probably Read had in mind the poem 'Coventry'. Heron wrote it after attending the opening of the new cathedral. Here is its first stanza –

Pain is in everything –
in joy, in love, in life,
(and even granite is alive).
Only death is painless
though the approach to it
sums up all pain.

Read didn't say whether he thought Heron had sufficiently polished any gems, but others did. A favourite is:

Good Friday

The world was made
by Love
for Love
and Love shall be.
Why then, the Tree?

The world is made
of Love
if Love
has eyes to see
Love on the Tree.

Most of his poems were looser; their essence was less concentrated, which rendered them accessible to a wider public. Such is the case with –

Take And Give

Greed loves to take and hates to give
and what it takes hoards in a sieve
that only holds what cannot live.

Pride tries to give and will not take
and what it 'gives' can only make
a sleeping pain come wide awake.

The model is the air we breathe
and then in thankfulness bequeath
to words that love and praise enwreathe.

As the years went by, Heron's poetry became a vehicle for a greater range of topic, embracing the natural world in a conservationist grasp. The telescopic in contrast to the microscopic mode produced 'Brack Ross Holiday,' an allegorical poem of over two hundred lines, seeing the glorious Kerry landscape in terms of the Anglican liturgy. Brack Ross was unique. Knowing that its author was eighty-four makes the last line all the more poignant: 'Tomorrow I go home.'

But tomorrow was not yet. The poetry bug was ineradicable though the gems were fewer. Inevitably, instead of drawing on new experiences, Heron was recycling old data. A poet may be self-indulgent and self-deceived. Some thought this was the case with the poem 'The Way of Life,' which began with the lines:

> Teach me O Lord to know I do not know
> Empty my mind of self my self of mind
> Mould and inform me in the vacuum
> that I may learn to orbit round the Word
> praising the sempiternal mystery
> The Word made flesh that came to dwell among us.

There were a few broadsides from friends over this poem. Frederic Osborn, pioneer of town and country planning and Heron's Welwyn Garden City friend, responded sharply. Was there not something fundamentally immoral about the poem?

'Briefly, my criticism would be that you pray to God to relieve you of thought and responsibility and take over your Self for your Self's own peace and satisfaction. Surely this is phony abdication that just puts your Self back on the throne with a mightier royal household. I don't see you as that sort of self-centred salvation seeker at all.'

Osborn subjoined an alternative draft Prayer for Heron.

> Truth, Take notice! Homo sum;
> Would-be host of Kingdom Come;
> Mend my Self's myopic Mind
> That a fresh vision I may find,
> And learn, with distance glasses on,
> If Kingdom Come has come and gone.
> Teach me the Word is but the seed:
> The Self is measured by the Deed!

This exchange illustrates both the limitations and the appeal of Heron's poetry across the divides of belief.

T.S. Eliot was a tremendous influence on Heron. It is well-known that Eliot refused to discuss his work. What he had written he had written. He declared more than once that a poem meant what the reader made of it. He wrote from and within his own experience. Then, like clay in the potter's hands, that experience, where tragedy intertwined with inspiration, was given shape and meaning. The poem coming to birth painfully was a self-emptying but not a discarding. The mind is both awful and awesome as a receptacle. The inexpressibly wonderful moments of life are inclined to slip through mind's mesh, leaving the body without the background, like fish struggling in a net after the water has disappeared, whilst the shadowy aspects of living remain in the mind, forgiven by others but not by ourselves and rarely forgotten.

Heron was no imitator of Eliot but the influence from Eliot's style is unmistakable. Yet Heron never quite learnt to let go of his poems. There was always a desire to share his poems with people. During the pregnancy, many eyes were invited to see the growing embryo and offer criticism and advice on the nurturing before birth. Like Eliot, Heron wanted to write the word that initiates, the word that leads to meanings. The weak who do not think will use the poetry of others as concluding words, bolstering up their half-baked ideas or hardening prejudices. Of good poetry the oft repeated words are true:

> I am not eager to rehearse
> My thoughts and theory which you have forgotten
> These things have served their purpose, let them be.

Heron could not 'let them be' in this way. He wrote from inner experience and wanted to share his experience and vision with others. He needed to know what other people thought of his poems – hence the preliminary circulation of drafts to friends with an invitation to respond. Improvements were made following advice given. When Eliot read a draft of 'Coventry' he wrote:

'I was much interested by your reaction to 'Coventry' and have read your poem a number of times. I hesitate to make any such decision about another man's verse, and if you yourself feel strongly that the last two lines are necessary to express your experience, that should decide it.'

Eliot continues:

'I should be inclined to end with 'where Christ is seen in Glory' though I think the name of Coventry comes in usefully – but I do feel a bit let down by 'sound God's triumph' after the impressiveness of the 'Glory.'

(Letter to Heron 7 July 1962).

The published poem ended:

> Pain takes its place in Coventry,
> is reconciled with life
> where Christ is seen in Glory.

Whatever more celebrated names had to offer, it was Heron's old, trusted, argumentative and proven Chandos friends who had the greatest influence on the progress of his poetry. Maurice Reckitt, Philip Mairet, Demant and Travers Symons offered line-by-line comment and criticism. Travers Symons' comments were particularly helpful, even if he did not think so, as they came from a non-churchman. Symons felt, wrongly, that he could not do justice to Heron's thought because, so

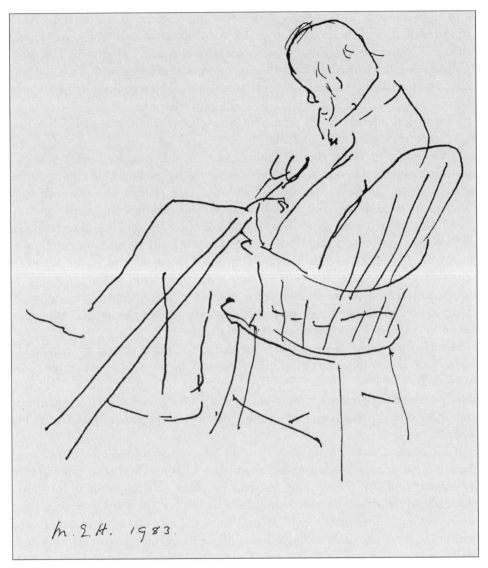

Tom Heron asleep in armchair, 1983 by Margaret Heron.

far as he had ground under his feet, it was different from the ground under Heron's. Symons had been entranced by Jesus Christ throughout his conscious life, but the Church that had been created in his name seemed to him, early in his life, to be just the sort of institution the Jewish form of which Jesus came to destroy. Symons thought the dwindling effect of the Church in the world was partly due to its excessive emphasis on the crucifixion suffering of Jesus, to the loss of his life's emphasis on the love of God and love of neighbour which he laid on the heart of man with the unending joy which that state of consciousness would release in the human soul.

In a poem such as 'Coventry', pain was pre-eminent. Some friendly critics wondered if the emphasis was too great. Was this a true expression of Heron's feeling? It seemed so negative, whereas most pain is a matter of growth. The petals of the flower wither that the seeds may ripen; human beings pass through the pain of sin and mistake to the happiness of clearer vision and less compelling wickedness. Pain is so much a matter of cost – but well worth paying.

Nonetheless, Heron was by temperament and conviction optimistic. There was more hope than fear in his outlook.

If Philip Mairet was a kindred spirit in ideas, it was Maurice Reckitt who had the most detailed influence on his poetry. Surviving papers show how whole passages of poems were altered in the light of Reckitt's 'blue pencil'. The two men were different in background, outlook and temperament. Heron's long-term views inclined him to take a far more hopeful outlook upon the political, economic and social order than Reckitt could, who thought man's predicament must continue to be, for the rest of the twentieth century, far more desperate than Heron anywhere suggested in his poems. The most difficult lesson for Heron to learn was how to express his ideas in poetry. It involved a tautness of writing and a pruning of the clutter-words which often help prose but in poetry weaken the impact. Also, there has to be a variation and interplay of rhythmic stress.

Heron's vision was so good that it needed to be made sharper on paper. His friends helped him to tighten his poems. Gradually he was able to impart his vision – an abiding legacy – in *Call it a Day*, a selection of thirty-six poems. Through these poems and the many as yet unpublished ones, the complete Heron is perceived and understood. As has been said already, Heron was not primarily a dreamer but an artist.

If his vision surfaces in his poems, so do his deepest convictions. In older age there is a more brooding, silent and meditative Heron. The restrictions imposed by reduced mobility and wavering eyesight provided more opportunity for prayer and daily introductions to new humilities. His life became a steady journey to a new beginning rather than a series of 'mea culpa's. The past was vivid and, having achieved so much, he could be forgiven for a slight enlargement of past achievements. He knew there had to be a degree of self-emptying before the end. It is more easily proposed than carried out. Heron knew that the day after tomorrow may be too late. He did not delay. He had to be ready, as expressed in one of his most memorable poems, for

The Great Day

Lord, give me time to die a healthy death,
the Church my midwife,
or fuse in fell absolvent flash
the scattered lights of long senectitude,
so either way my deathday may exalt
the dignity of man.

Eulalie also had to be prepared. Of the last stage of their journey together she was to write to John Peart-Binns:

'I was aware for some time past that I could not hope to keep him with me much longer. His life had grown so thin – except internally, he said to me not long before he went into hospital with the head shingles – "I am glad I have learned to meditate".'

Tom Heron's Great Day came on 11th November 1983.

Interlogue

THIS FINAL CHAPTER PROVIDES both an epilogue to the biography and a prologue to the selection of writings that follows; in fact a bridge between them. It attempts to answer blunt and basic questions. Why should the Millennium reader be interested in a largely unknown businessman brought up in late Victorian and Edwardian England? Do not the host of changes in technology and science, in the patterns of culture and everyday life, and even in the physical environment itself, render the problems Heron wrestled with both obsolete and irrelevant? To some extent the subjective question of interest will have answered itself already one way or another. Suffice it here to add that since few people who met Tom Heron ever forgot him, there is reason to hope that enough of his charisma has been captured in these pages for it to operate posthumously.

Heron's relevance today, on the other hand, needs explanation, for it is both complex and as yet largely unrecognized. It has two dimensions. One relates to the past and depends upon the extent to which knowledge of Heron's life and achievement helps us to understand how things became what they did and to a lesser degree what they are. As a small piece of social history, Heron's story may add colour to movements already known about, making them more real and memorable, because social history touches public imagination most powerfully when presented in terms of individual people rather than in abstract generalizations.

The second dimension relates to the present and the near future. It depends on the extent to which Heron's experience and ideas may help today's society to understand the nature of problems facing it so that wiser decisions and courses of action can be taken, or, conversely so that certain false trails can be abandoned. Even during his lifetime, he was regarded at times as something of a 'prophet', not in any sense of foretelling the future but in directing attention to truths about the nature of man and society which will have to be accommodated in any future system of economy and industry if it is to achieve long-term satisfaction.

There are many reasons why comparatively little of Heron's writing is out of date at the turn of the century. Perhaps the most important is his deep distrust of the superficial and the short-term in any field. His instinct and habit was to delve to the roots of a matter, looking for permanent solutions based on lasting, if not eternal, values. So although he was constantly making practical decisions for immediate implementation, they were made within a long-term perspective and he avoided commitment to dogmatic positions which would close the door to fresh understanding and adaptation as situations changed. This left him free to disengage if time or circumstance indicated that a policy no longer promised to deliver, as in the case of his interest in Social Credit. It also meant that even when the details of one of his proposals ceased to be appropriate, the principles were often seen to be sound and worth re-dressing. He did not often need to recant so much as review.

Thus it is not the details of the many causes which Heron argued so forcefully that is of potential relevance to later decades, but the underlying ideas he was expressing and his example of measuring mundane, day-to-day policies against the deepest-held values. In Heron's case these values were essentially and explicitly those of Christian culture, but that in no way limits his relevance to self-acknowledged Christian communities or individuals. Indeed, throughout his lifetime, many of the greatest admirers of his business practice and morality held quite different faiths.

A second characteristic helping to explain Heron's continuing relevance is his balance and moderation. Though he expressed himself graphically and forcefully, the typical tenor of his argument was seldom extreme. He rarely believed that one side was entirely right and the other entirely wrong. His readiness to recognize whatever merit he could discern in those whose policies he opposed and even detested (the apartheid leaders in South Africa spring to mind) permeated his speeches and writing with a tolerance and charity which is too often lacking nowadays. This lack of dogmatism left him with a more diverse, and therefore a wider, audience than many thinkers enjoy. For example Trade-Unionists and traditional socialists can appreciate Heron's work as the acceptable face of capitalism, while captains of industry can recognize that unlike many reformers, Heron was sufficiently one of themselves to be worth listening to.

Even in the first flush of his Fabian enthusiasm, Heron never doubted the enormous potential usefulness of the human inventions of money and the capitalist system. Nor was he for long, if ever, ready to place the weal of the nation on the altar of total state control. (see Appendix p. 155) His middle way was as firmly pragmatic as it was principled. His balancing act was tested year in, year out, in the welter of petty, as well as major, decisions which it is the lot of business managers to resolve. Over the question of state control, the pendulum has swung dramatically throughout the twentieth century. It is still swinging and it could be that while it continues to swing, the debate may carry echoes of Heron's voice.

Yet another reason why much of Heron's writings have been slow to 'date' derives from his own evergreen interest in whatever was new. Besides being an innovator himself, he remained open to new developments almost to the end of his life, and took special notice of movements captivating the young. For example, in his eighties he was actively supporting Schumacher's Intermediate (Appropriate) Technology. When over ninety he was urging his son to join the New Village Association, having joined it himself. To his mind, change for the better was always possible, which helps to explain why much of his writing remains compatible with subsequent events.

All but three of the appendices were written by Heron and one of those exceptions is a report of what he said. A majority of the items written after 1961 in his seventies are examples of his poetry, whereas the appendices before that date constitute examples of his serious contributions to public debate on social and economic issues. It is in these, the earlier writings, that evidence is most likely to be found of the continuing relevance of Heron's thinking.

It is important that these appendices are not construed as complete statements of the cases Heron was making. They are extracts only, from writings which are themselves selected from a larger body of work. Their strength and weakness lies, as it always lay, in being the fruit of experience in a pressured business career that never gave him the time or peace for prolonged meditation or scholarly organization; not that it is clear what use he would have made of such time and peace had he been granted them.

The weaknesses of this method, if such it should be called, are easily imagined. The price he paid in incomplete lines of thought, missing or inaccurate references and even inconsistencies, brought an immediacy of focus on whatever he most wanted to say. What mattered most to Heron at the time, and what still matters most today, is whether his writing sowed seeds of truth which others could reap and not whether critics could find scope to use their blue pencils.

A quick gallop through the appendices will reveal the following as themes Heron felt compelled to air: consumer power in general and the potential of Christian consumers in particular; the greater importance of practical over dogmatic consider-ations in the debate about state control; the importance of quality and purpose in evaluating employment and unemployment; the link between the individual's responsibility and the operation of good government; incentives to work and 'shares' for miners and other workers; the modern leisure heresy and the relationship between leisure and work; automation and unemployment; how to use the fruit of increased productivity; the survival of personal and creative work beyond death; a 'Labour Reserve' – a new name and policy to cope with redundancies; different rhythms of work and the combination of rest and effort in work; prayer and science.

The above list should indicate that the central themes of Heron's social concern by no means belong to the past alone. On the contrary, it appears that after some thirty years in which the economic/industrial/commercial life of the nation swung away from the values Heron championed, the tide has begun to turn again. Most if not all of the subjects listed can be found under fresh scrutiny as the new century opens. In commerce and environmental matters in particular, there are signs of the weakening of enslavement to 'the bottom line' – the very phrase epitomizes the spiritual poverty of the period that accepts it as axiomatic! It is increasingly conceded in certain areas of the economy that there is a place for other than monetary incentives and measurements even within our prevailingly materialistic culture.

In so far as this change of climate persists, Heron's message seems more likely to find a sympathetic hearing than in recent decades. For the assumption that the age of modern science and technology had left human barbarism behind can no longer be held with confidence while pictures of atrocities in every continent are beamed on to the television screens in our living rooms. Paradoxically it is a technological triumph, the information revolution, that forces modern society to face up once again to man's apparently ineradicable capacity for brutality, even towards the defenceless and the innocent.

Heron wrestled all his life to reconcile social and economic policy with some explanation of the coexistence of good and evil. He could only find and express optimism in terms of traditional Christian metaphor. That language, like his colloquialisms, may be unfamiliar to many and an obstacle to some, but it does not mask or distort the drift of his arguments, which will get through to people already addressing the same or kindred problems.

During his life Heron was recognized for his integration of religious and material disciplines, the ideal and the pragmatic, the desirable and the possible. The lack of public balance between these elements since his death has helped to relegate him to the company of the irrelevant or the forgotten. If his experience and thought are found significant in future, it will be on two accounts. First for the way in which his general approach is validated by events because it is seen to be based on true observations of the nature of man and of society; second, for what he has to say about the nature and purpose of work.

It is necessary to stress this last aspect of Heron's thought, not just because it provides a thread running through his whole life, informing all the other elements of his philosophy and practice, but because of its originality. Few people in modern times will have thought so long and deeply about this basic, universal human activity, and striven so consistently to put the conclusions of that thought into industrial and commercial practice. It is half a century since Heron described what he called the 'modern heresy of leisure' (Appendix see p. 162), built on the assumption that the less work, the better. There is still a need for a social philosophy that incorporates a positive attitude to work, recognizing it as an essential ingredient of spiritual life. This assertion is not a reactionary defence of the Protestant work ethic of yester-year, not of work as a medicine, the efficacy of which is related to unpleasantness. Work for Heron was not a duty but a means of releasing talents and expressing relationships. For him the patterns to follow were those of the artist and the family, not in the sense of the painter and the couple with 2.4 children, but as metaphors for activity and relationships which enable people to find fulfilment and contentment in service, so that they can lose themselves in their work.

The following appendices are offered, therefore, in the belief that they have something to offer a society in which work is tending to become a privilege instead of a common birthright; in which wealth is sought by lottery unrelated to effort or merit; in which security is sought in isolation guarded by closed-circuit television and big dogs; in which the sense of community gives way to looking after number one; in which the quality of life is sacrificed to the postponement of death.

From 'Christian Vocation in Industry and Marketing'

Published in 1926 as one of a series of Anglo-Catholic Congress Books

Prefaced by Bishop Gore

WE HAVE BECOME SO USED TO REGARDING CHRISTIANITY as a religion which has no message for the Economist, that we have forgotten how enormous is the economic power in the hands of Christians.

This economic power will never be rightly or fruitfully used until the Christian doctrine of ownership is properly understood and taught. That doctrine is, of course, founded upon the idea expressed in the familiar term 'stewardship'. This must not be taken to mean that the possession of wealth, however acquired, or however concentrated in a few hands, can none-the-less be justified if it is expended in a careful and benevolent fashion. What it does mean is that when a man has satisfied himself that his property has not come to him from any discreditable source, and has been fairly earned as far as he had had the opportunity to earn it, he has still to remember that he holds it in trust for God, to whom in due course the account must be rendered. The Church has not so far offered to the faithful much guidance in this important respect. Yet if it is true that the principles and conditions of an explicitly Christian industry can be discovered (as it is here contended), and if again it is true that there is sufficient capital in the possession of whole-hearted Christian people adequately to finance schemes based thereupon (as seems certainly to be the case), then a real opportunity lies before us of mobilizing the economic power which is now in Christian hands for the greater glory of God and the true happiness of society. Wealth now under the control of Christians can set in operation and make actual the Christian ideals of vocation and fellowship in industry, the Christian tradition of good craftsmanship in work, and the Christian doctrines of the Just Price. So will the maker be freed, and the user be truly served.

The Area of the Market

Most of a Letter Published in
G.K.'s Weekly, July 16th, 1927

SIR, -
Eric Gill's trenchant criticism of Father Vincent McNabb's pamphlet has given me unalloyed pleasure. When first I read that 'things should be produced where they can be most economically consumed,' I thought for a moment that Father Knox was up to another of his tricks. The phrase had the right look about it. I read it aloud. It sounded all right. But when I tried to fit hand block printed silks into it I felt that the new principle would have to be stated in Latin before it would convey anything to me. If Father Knox is not involved, I do hope an answer will be forthcoming to Eric Gill's question, 'How are things economically consumed?' And if there should prove to be some special virtue in Economic Consumption, whatever it is, I should like to know if there is any special reason why things should not be economically consumed where they are produced. (I'm hanged if I'll leave Cornwall to be near a mere consumer.) Besides, if hand block printed silks are most economically consumed in Merthyr Tydvill or Oldham – the phrase suggests this dreadful possibility – and therefore have to be produced in one of those towns, I am afraid that even the dwellers in that town will soon cease to buy them. Perhaps after all that is what Father Vincent McNabb is driving at. Perhaps consumption can be so economical that no production whatever will be required to meet it. Much as I deplore the senseless carting about of rubbish which this age calls business, I hope that the urge to produce is not to be taken away from us.

But no craftsman cares a rap when you tell him that he ought not to work in the place he has selected as being the best suited for his work, or that people ought to buy ugly things merely because they are made in their own village.

T. M. Heron.

The Rhythm of Work

Two passages from Heron's unfinished book (1941)

I. St Ives Fishermen

WALKING PAST THE HARBOUR soon after I went to live at St Ives, I saw the fishing boats arrive. The skipper and hands brought the boat to shore and then strode off to get breakfast and a rest. It was the women, assisted by the younger men, who unloaded the fish, and it was the women who counted the fish and received the money for it. The similarity between the division of labour in the Yorkshire Dales and in this Cornish fishing town struck me immediately. Here the men were generally to be seen smoking their pipes and leaning over the harbour rails gazing out to sea. Those who had been away with the trawlers would pace backwards and forwards, four paces each way, whilst yarning away at one another. Occasionally a boat would have to be caulked and painted, and that was, of course, man's job. But even the work of drying and mending the nets was shared by the women. Certainly the women gossiped among themselves, but nearly always they were working with their hands at the same time. In addition to helping the men with their work, they looked after their cottages and their children, made their men's clothes, and either took in visitors or helped at the boarding houses during the summer. And as in my old village, they did most of the public worshipping. But one night I went out with the herring fleet and then I saw the St Ives men really at work. It was as though they had been husbanding their strength so that they could put forth the utmost effort when God sent the herrings. Desultory fishing was a worthy occupation which kept your eye in and brought a little money, but the job to which these men had given themselves was that of hunting the herring when in due season the shoals appeared.

It was my work amidst the St Ives fisher folk which made me realise that there was a natural rhythm about all work, that the tempo of the rhythm was decided by the kind of job that was being done, and that generally speaking there was a different rhythm about a woman's work from that of a man. And my marriage and my experience as a father of a family contributed to this discovery.

II Rest and Effort

I REALISED THAT WHEN A MAN SAWS PROPERLY, he breathes in as he pulls and releases his breath as he lets his partner pull the saw back. Brace and relax, effort and rest, formed the pattern of the rhythm of the saw. Obviously this was true of rowing and swimming as well. The idea that there was rest in work, not merely after it, struck me as an important fact. I remembered how I had discovered the opposite truth – that work was inherent in rest. One hot summer's day I had set off by myself and climbed to the top of Whernside. For a long time I had lain perfectly still looking out over the wide expanse which hid Dent and Gawthrop and Sedbergh. Everywhere was rest and repose, but as I looked and meditated, the stillness seemed pulsing with energy: myriads of physics told me about the tremendous forces required to keep a single atom from disintegrating. Here around me was visual confirmation of energy in repose, the quivering of the landscape akin to the quivering of the tight-rope walker or ballet dancer whose controlled balance looks so effortless. According to the physicists, the universe itself is but the balance maintained by a vast interplay of forces, energy at work throughout the cosmos. This idea of the universe being always at work, at once brings God into the picture, even if you only call him the eternal worker without whom the physical world would not hold together. God always at work in the world, man made in the image of God – these thoughts passed through my mind as I remembered that I myself could only keep from disintegrating by constantly making efforts. Having in my early manhood discovered that rest is always dependent on work, it was not until middle age that I realised that in practice my best work was always the result of a combination of rest and effort; that in fact there was always rest in work; that the right sort of work, so to speak, financed itself.

I could understand why my farmer friend had always appeared so right when he was merely looking over a gate. He (or his forebears) had won the field from the moor, and had walled it and drained it. He had taken his hay off it and manured it in due season, and now, having turned his cattle into it, he had only to watch God carrying on with the good work. He was working in partnership with nature; sometimes it was his turn to make the effort, sometimes he could leave it to nature. There was a long interval between some of the stresses of the rhythm which ran through the upland farmer's work, but it was unmistakably a rhythm. 'I've ten acres of potatoes working for me in Low Fold', said one farmer as we drank in the inn parlour at noon.

'The Relation of Freedom and Control in Industry'

Four extracts from Heron's pamphlet published by the Industrial Christian Fellowship, in 1943

Consumer Control

THE FIRST THING TO NOTICE ABOUT CONSUMER CONTROL is that the consumer is rarely allowed to see what industry is actually doing. He is merely confronted with the finished product and told that he may take it or leave it. But neither the consumer nor anyone else can effectively control an activity about which he is being kept in ignorance. Our factories and workshops must therefore be thrown open to the public gaze, so that anyone interested can find out how the things he will be asked to buy are being made.

The Consumer's use of money

LET US NOW CONSIDER THE PART WHICH MONEY PLAYS in enabling the consumer to control industry. I often think that our attention is so much directed to the faults of the monetary system that we are inclined to forget how important an instrument it is for giving to the individual consumer the opportunity to exercise his freedom as a consumer. But the possessor of money, by having the option to spend it on one thing rather than on another, is not only thereby given a limited power to live his life as he wants to, he is also given, in the direction of his purchases, a limited control over the industry which serves him. This control is at present vitiated, partly because all too often money is used irresponsibly, and partly because, in the vast majority of cases, the individual consumer possesses too little money to enable him adequately to express his taste and discrimination in his purchasing. I do not know whether true industry suffers more from the lack of money available for the consumption of its products than it does from the misdirection of the money which is already available. Both evils must be tackled. To some extent effective demand would be made to approximate more to the call for what the good life required if a few people had very much less money to spend than they now have and the many people had far more.

Management as a Vocation

I AM AWARE THAT ANY PROPOSAL for taking the blinkers off industry will meet with opposition from many of the interests concerned, and if injustice is not to be done, we may have to proceed by interim measures accompanied by schemes of compensation. But the principle is clear and we ought to work towards it. And in doing so, I think we shall have the support of the men who, no matter what we do, are really going to have a very big say in shaping our future – the artist technicians. I give this title to the type of man who, having a vision of new things to be made or new ways of making them, cannot rest or let other people rest until he realises his vision in practice.

If we do not give this man his proper freedom, he will kick over the traces. If we do, he will help us to make management 'earn its keep,' for the creative function, which alone makes management honourable and justifies its privileges, is that of providing conditions under which men may work as freemen, exercising initiative and restraint as new knowledge about processes or new expressions of consumer taste have to be taken into account. It is the job of management to graft new methods on to old systems, and to do so with the least possible disturbance to the consumer whilst the change is taking place. We shall, I think, tend to get the right managers if we concentrate on seeing that businesses are run properly, rather than on seeing that they are owned properly, for the ownership we really want is in each case that which enables the right process to be carried out. By plumping for public ownership or standing pat for private, we merely postpone consideration of the more fundamental and difficult question.

State Control

THIS BRINGS US TO THE VEXED QUESTION OF STATE CONTROL. Here I think our main trouble is that at the moment we have only a confused idea about what the State's function in the industrial field ought to be. In consequence, such directions as the State gives tend to be either timid or dictatorial. Yet in spite of this, State control has many achievements to its credit and in wartime is regarded as indispensable. But the point to be noted about Government control in wartime is that, no matter how dictatorial it may be, it is accepted, not because the majority of people have a passionate desire to serve the State, but because they feel that for the time being the State is strenuously engaged in serving them; it is defending them against the worst of all possible controls – that imposed by a foreign State.

Whether in peacetime any State can evoke similar loyalty is open to doubt. The enthusiasm of the Russians for the Soviet Government was at any rate partially due to the fact that the rest of the world was arrayed against it. What is certain, however, is that the worker's strongest instinct is to serve his work. It matters less to him whether he is working for the State or not than whether his work goes well or not. If the work goes better under national ownership, well and good. If it does not, the fact that the worker is one forty-millionth part of the State will not reconcile him either to misdirection or to exploitation.

Obviously the State must own and direct its fighting machine, for in that case the State is the only consumer of the product – only the State may wage war. But in general there is an unanswerable argument against the State assuming direct charge in any industry. For if the State is the producer, who then is to control the producer? The State's true function is to see that justice is done, on the one hand between producer and consumer, and on the other between one producer and another.

A Balance of Controls.

INDUSTRY IS A LIVING THING and its technique constantly outgrows the laws we make for it. Nevertheless its practice must be controlled by laws, some of which ought to be made by a managing director or works committee and some by the State. But in all cases we ought to ask of the controller or law-maker precisely what it is that he wants his rule to bring about, for it is only when we know what an industrial control is supposed to do that we can begin to judge whether it is legitimate or even effective. And in the same way that we ask the controller, 'What is your control for?', so with regard to every claim for freedom we ought to ask 'What is your freedom for?' A demand for freedom may upon analysis prove to be either a despicable request for power to exploit others or, what is a very different matter, a praiseworthy insistence upon one's right to follow one's vocation and make a thing as it should be made. There is no more abused word in our vocabulary than the word 'Freedom'.

Full Employment Policy

Part of Heron's critique in the New English Weekly was reprinted as a pamphlet entitled 'Prolegomena to the Methodology of the Study of Unnecessary Sweat.'

BEFORE THE WAR OUR SOCIETY SUFFERED from the effects of mass unemployment. There is no doubt that this unemployment was a bad thing. Therefore its opposite, Full Employment, must be a good thing. So, in effect, say the politicians. But the truth of the matter is that the good which results from employment is never determined solely by the amount of employment which exists. The benefits which employment can give depend, in the main, upon the quality of the work which is being done, and upon the direction which that work is taking.

In England, we based our industrial system upon a reserve of penalized unemployed. Against all reason, and with perverse obstinacy, we insisted that most men should actually be worse off the moment they had finished making whatever they were making! In Germany, they based their Nazi system upon the desperate belief that the best employment for any man was one dictated for him by a super-man. If, in either country, a genuine attempt had been made to *share* whatever labours the proper use of the machine entails, if such an attempt had been inspired by the determination to make the structure of industry serve man's spiritual urge to employ himself, the crisis in our civilization could hardly have taken the violent turn it has done. And no military success, however complete, can dispose of that crisis.

Good employment produces good results. Bad employment produces bad results. To maximize bad employment is merely to add to the scale of our distress.

Employment exists for the sake of unemployment. Even bad employment exists for the sake of bad unemployment; in which term can be included the idleness of those who enjoy the fruits of industrial leadership, whilst evading its responsibilities. The good unemployment for which the good employment exists is what the word 'leisure' used to denote. It is the time *allowed* for the enjoyment of work on which we have already expended our labour. It is the time available for walking the earth and choosing responsibly the next good thing there is to do. That is the norm – to work as the artist works.

We are now trying to organize Full Employment – although we have not the slightest idea what kind of life we want that employment to give!

1945

National Day of Prayer July 6th 1946

Extracts from BBC Home Service
written and spoken by Heron conducting the service

THE VITAL CONNECTION BETWEEN OUR OWN INDIVIDUAL WORK and our politics has got lost! Unless people who draw up national plans and peace treaties do their work well, it makes it much harder for us to do ours – sometimes impossible! But the opposite is just as true. Unless we do our work well, theirs is bound to suffer. We depend on them and they depend on us. And just now, God knows, they need our help.

If this is so, let us remember that we can't even criticize their plans constructively unless by honest work of our own, we have won for ourselves decent values by which we can measure what they propose to do for us.

And what is even more important, let us remember, that since we are truly 'all members one of another,' to the extent that we learn to pray rightly about our own particular jobs and do them properly, to that extent we help our leaders and governors to pray rightly and act wisely in theirs.

I look first at my own trade. I am a manufacturer. Are the goods which I manufacture the kind of goods which I would like to have for my own use, or for the use of my friend?

In my business I am both a buyer and a seller. Do I always try to buy at a price which I would think to be a fair price if I were the seller? And when I am a seller do I always try to sell at a price which I would think fair if I myself were having to buy?

I am responsible for the way certain processes have to be carried out. Is each process the one I would want to use if I were doing the job myself? Are the working conditions those I would choose for my own son or daughter?

Then what about other manufacturers in my line of business? Am I doing anything to help them to prosper as I myself would prosper?

And finally, am I respecting God's Natural Creation, am I caring enough for the raw materials which his bounty has provided, and for the natural surroundings in which my works are set? And am I matching this respect for the Natural Universe (which even a good Pantheist would show) with an even greater respect for the nature which God has implanted in man? Am I really trying to help as many people as possible to find the particular jobs for which their special skills and aptitudes fit them? In short, am I working for my own personal power and security, or am I honestly trying to fulfil my vocation and help other men to fulfil theirs?

Those are the kind of questions I ask myself. We can each of us draw up a similar list about the particular work we happen to do. Is there any doubt that, to the extent that we do ask ourselves such questions, and respond to them as Christians should, to that extent we create the very stuff of which Peace is made. We spread Christian fellowship, and on that our Statesmen and organisers can build and build well.

Incentives to Work

Christian News Letter 1947

WE SHALL BEGIN BY CONSIDERING A CASE where the natural inducements and compulsions direct the work of the community in its most perfect form – a human family isolated from the rest of mankind and left to fend for itself amidst surroundings which offer opportunities for human survival.

Obviously the father, the mother and the children, each person according to his strength and ability, will be called upon to share the work which will be necessary if all are to be fed and sheltered. They will have to co-operate. And whatever co-operation is achieved will be found to derive from inducements and penalties which Nature provides. The joy of achievement, the fear of failure; the pleasure of giving, the distaste for having to beg; the interest in an experiment, the dissatisfaction with inadequate tools; the warmth of a fire, the deadening effect of the cold; the sight of someone happily lost in a job of work, the emptiness of feeling that one has nothing to do; the desire of the scholar to learn, the fear of the experienced lest his hard-won knowledge should not be passed on; the pride of real ownership, the disgrace of having neglected what was entrusted to one's care; the anticipation of a feast, the dread of inadequate diet; all these and a thousand other considerations pull and prod man to his work, and to the extent that they do so in right and ordered measure, the work of this family will be likely to prosper.

To own a forty-millionth part of the pit one is working in cannot really give much satisfaction to anyone; and the negative satisfaction, that the capitalist no longer owns it, is no substitute for real ownership. Even under a system of National Control and State Ownership of Mineral Rights, it should be possible to allot Labour Shares in individual pits to the miners who are working in them. These Shares should be issued in proportion to the stakes which the miners have risked – the number of years worked and the value of the work done.

An excessive emphasis upon 'output' is bound to produce, in addition to the goods planned for, social consequences which weaken the life of the community. When unemployed miners were starving in the Welsh valleys, many of those who remained in the pits were compelled to work at a pace which was quite inhuman. For every extra ton of coal then won, many more have since been lost, because, by winning the Coal, we lost the Man.

Past neglect of the mines and mining villages leaves us owing the mining community a debt. On the one hand, a mining village as well designed as Welwyn Garden City would make men want to find work in their own town; on the other hand, wonderful new labour-saving machinery and equipment (designed for oper-ations which the inventors themselves would want to carry out 'in that way') would make men *want* to live in the town where that machinery was available for their use. And, since our landscape gardeners have no longer the Squire's parkland to operate upon, why cannot they be allowed to experiment with the tips and waste lands which surround our pits, continually reminding all who see them of our past rapacity?

What has Christianity to say to Leisure in the Modern State?

Extracts from the Industrial Christian Fellowship pamphlet, being the substance of Heron's address in Southwark Cathedral 20th May 1949

I SHOULD LIKE TO BEGIN BY DESCRIBING what I think we Christians ought to be calling the Modern Leisure Heresy. I think it runs something like this. We have discovered that by equipping ourselves with labour-saving machinery, and by organizing production on a large scale, we can produce more things in less time than our forefathers were ever able to do. It is taken for granted that this in itself is a good thing, and it is assumed that if only we can go on learning how to produce more and more things in less and less time, then soon we shall all be living in a state of plenty, and have lots of free time, and that will be splendid. If today we are more often aware of austerity than of plenty, the excuse given is that we are suffering from the destruction and dislocation caused by the war. And by many the inherent wickedness of the Russians, or of the Financiers, or of the Jews, is thought to make some postponement of the leisure age inevitable. But in the nature of things, this is what leisure is now supposed to be – freedom from work and from the curse of work; time to enjoy the contents of the bigger and better barns, when we have built and stored them. And the general assumption is that if only we are sensible and good, we shall put up with the unpleasant tasks which a machine economy imposes, and find ourselves richly compensated for any loss of freedom in our work by having our leisure hours extended; the bargain is believed to be too good to be missed.

Our trouble is, I think, that because we have left religion out of account, we have landed ourselves with two quite irrational concepts, the one of work, the other of something which is merely not work, which we call leisure. Is a bored shop assistant, waiting for customers who do not come, really working? Is a university blue, rowing harder than galley slave ever rowed, not working? But accepting for the moment our popular concepts of work and leisure, is it not clear that as it is always a human person who carries over from the one activity into the other, any defect in a work activity is bound to affect a leisure activity adversely?

Unless we can get our work right, we cannot possibly get our leisure right. If we have a bad conscience about our work or a feeling of grievance about it, any holiday which we take is bound to be but a temporary escape from work. All the time we are having our so-called holiday, the cloud of our work will be hanging over us. And under these circumstances we shall be tempted to force our holiday into a hectic and unnatural shape. Is not this the explanation of the fact that after so many holidays today people find it more difficult than ever to resume their everyday occupations?

If our work does not satisfy us, the place to remedy matters is in the work itself, not outside it. And if our mass production processes exert a de-naturalizing and de-personalizing influence upon us, then it is our mass production processes which we must alter. We have the means to do so.

Will Automation cause Unemployment?

Extracts from an Industrial Christian Fellowship
pamphlet, October 1957

IF WE CAN AVOID WARS AND COMMOTIONS AND PULL TOGETHER, our machinery will enable us to produce more goods in the same amount of time, or the same amount of goods in less time, than we have hitherto been doing. This means that within limits, which should expand if we use our knowledge and resources aright, we shall be free to choose between greater material wealth on the one hand, and on the other, more free time or leisure in which to enjoy our wealth. What we shall probably choose is a bit of both – we are in fact already doing so.

Nevertheless we are still living in a society in which most of us have to sell our labour if we are to enjoy a reasonable standard of living, and we have no guarantee that a modern economy, when it is fighting for its existence, will not be as ruthless in its dealings with the individual as our forefathers were in the days of the first Industrial Revolution. Nor can we be certain that we shall be able to pass from the old order to the new without at some stage encountering economic difficulties which will put our humanity to the test.

Now, whilst employment is fairly stable, we ought to be making our plans to share as fairly as possible not only the gains, but also the losses, which may fall to our lot as a community whilst the new order is taking shape.

Certainly we must take every step we can to provide whatever employment is socially and economically desirable, but having done this, our next move should be to turn with even greater vigour to the question of what we can do with and for those who are thrown out of work by the new and superior work processes. At present, just because the unemployed form such a small proportion of the working population, we tend to forget their plight. Each one of the unemployed is a human person and our brother; and, on a lower plane of argument, how do we know that it may not be our turn next? We believe that now, whilst the going is still fairly good, is the proper time to improve our arrangements for re-training, rehabilitating in new neighbourhoods, and generally providing for the people who, in increasing numbers, ought to be displaced from their present jobs if we really use our new technical knowledge aright. We believe further that only as we do this, shall we succeed in providing our new industries with stable markets for the goods and services which really satisfy our human needs; for the goods and services the unemployed man and his family require for their well-being do not differ from those which the rest of us require. We shall deal at greater length with this question of the unemployed man in our answer to the question on leisure – the free time allowed to us as a result of our successful work time – and we shall insist that opportunities for leisure, like those for work, must be shared by all sections of the community. What we would emphasize at this stage is that, since technological unemployment proceeds from our strength and not from our weakness, the provisions we make for its victims should be on a much more generous scale than the help we now give to our unemployed.

A Fable

From Canon Demant's report on the 1957 Church Union
Summer School on the subject 'Christian Living in an
Expanding Economy'

ON THE LAST EVENING, Mr T. M. Heron, Director of Cresta Silks, summed
up. Instead of merely repeating what had been said by the speakers, he gave
his own interpretation of the implications of what had been said, in the form of
a fable or fairy tale, about uneconomic man, who values time more than money
and decided, in the fable, to keep the standard of living and productivity at what
it is in, say, 1957, and, in the future to use increased productivity not to increase
the amounts of goods produced, but to decrease the amount of time worked.
Uneconomic man in the fable of the future, starts work at twenty, and works
thirty-six hours a week. At twenty-one, he works thirty-five hours a week and so
on, throughout his working life, but drawing the usual increments due to his
seniority and made possible by ever increasing mechanization. By the time he is
fifty-five, he is only working for an hour a week and has all the rest of his time
for creative leisure or service.

A phantasy, said Mr Heron, but he went on to describe the leisure-time activities
that mechanization and its consequent relief from drudgery have made possible in
the industries near his home. Two large firms share an annual sports event and
require two big marquees to display the leisure-time products of their employees,
horticulture, wine-making, painting, furniture, metal-work, model engineering,
much of it work of a high standard, and none of it would have been thought
possible a hundred years ago.

From Heron's Address at the Funeral of John Baird

At Digswell Church Sept 1958. Baird's tragic, sudden death occurred only a year after he became Headmaster of Sherrardswood School

FROM HOLY SCRIPTURE AND FROM THE WRITINGS of saintly men living generations apart from one another, has been arranged and set before us what amounts to an explanation of what death means to the Christian. Each one of us as he goes about his daily work is constantly being given cause to remember that his own life on earth must some day come to an end. But as we pass a funeral cortège in the street, or glance down the obituary column in our morning newspaper, most of us instinctively switch our thoughts back to other things as quickly as we possibly can. We do this because our very nature responds with awe – with wonder mingled with fear – whenever we are actually brought face to face with death, and awe is incompatible with what we normally regard as comfort.

But this shrinking away from death, however natural it may be, is something which the Christian man turns to good account, for his meditation upon the one perfect death – the death upon the cross – has shown him that hope as well as fear is to be found in the mystery, and that the right hope, once found, ultimately banishes the fear.

Just as we know that Christ is alive today, and that His work continues, so we know that in some form or other the friend we mourn lives on, and the creative work he did, which was really inseparable from himself, lives on too. This is what the words of our Memorial Service convey to us in a language directed to a deeper level of consciousness than that to which reason alone can appeal, and it is against this background that I wish to say a few words to you tonight about John Barnet Baird.

Justice for the Unemployed

Extract from a manuscript entitled c. 1959

Heron proposed the 'redundant' be re-labelled 'Labour Reserve' and receive state aid of 'Half Pay' as a compromise between unemployment pay and the average wage.

IT WAS BECAUSE PERHAPS SUBCONSCIOUSLY we wanted to lessen the alarm caused by the use of the word 'unemployment' that the term 'redundant' came into common use; for if our labour power redounds, is superabundant, in excess of our needs, if new processes enable us to provide for our wants without having to sweat so hard, that is a sign that we are being Blessed! But this cheerful interpretation of redundancy cannot possibly retain its significance if to get the sack because you are redundant carries with it exactly the same penalties as to get the sack because you are inefficient or lazy! And as far as the State is concerned, that is the position of affairs today, for it is left to the charity (or the far-sightedness) of the individual employer to determine what (if any) compensation is paid to workers who lose their employment as a result of our developing production techniques. The implication of this failure to provide legal safeguards for the redundant worker is, of course, that as far as the rest of us are concerned, the whole man is redundant and not merely the labour which he used to give to a particular process; and all our existing schemes for retraining and rehabilitating have not prevented this unfortunate interpretation of redundancy from being accepted by those who are the chief victims of our technological victories. The names we give to people and to groups of people are important. This pamphlet is therefore a plea for such a re-assessment of unemployment as will lead to the recognition of the unemployed person for what he or she mostly is, in this age of great productivity – a member of the Labour Reserve. It is a plea for a Labour Reserve which, on the one hand, any civilized community might be proud of, and which on the other hand any member of the community might serve in without loss of status or physical well-being.

Towards the Redemption of Science

Two passages from a paper dated June 1960

PROFESSOR SODDY, WHO ASSISTED RUTHERFORD in his mathematical calculations, greeted the splitting of the atom with the remark that the new power at the disposal of mankind was sufficient to enable us to make a garden of Eden on a world scale, and this kind of potentiality was in the mind of Rutherford himself, who was reading *The Testament of Beauty* just before he made the final arrangements for his experiment. The creative scientist does pray about his work, and his discoveries about the workings of the natural creation are in a very real sense the answer to his prayers. In like manner the creative technologist, or businessman, or artist, or statesman prays about his work and is answered in it. But if all these individual workers pray about their work they do not all pray to the same God, or if it is the same God, they pray to different aspects of him, mistaking one aspect for the whole. It is for this reason that what may have been divine in the aim of the scientist is so often unrecognized or inadequately recognized by the technologist who is unduly concentrating upon another aspect of God. And from this confusion of prayers proceeds that confusion in the world which assails our very sanity. Yet from the achievement of our scientific disciplines there arises a recognition, as yet inadequately expressed, that every problem is a problem about God, for every discipline is related to every other.

The Christian surveying this scene is in no doubt about the remedy. The one power which can unify the divergent prayers of our creative workers is the power of Christ in whom all things are united. This statement is, of course, quite meaningless to the scientist who is also an unbeliever, and neither intellectual argument nor new discovery made in his own particular field can be relied upon to enlighten him. Nevertheless, either a new discovery or an argument may serve to disabuse him of some of the barriers which bar his way to belief. Moreover, his passion for objective truth, his contempt for the lie, and his awareness that the work to which he has dedicated himself is not proving an unmixed blessing – all these factors predispose him to make the gamble which is faith.

It may be said that a scientist is engaged upon establishing the facts about things and that prayer cannot alter a single fact. But are there not an illimitable number of facts to be found out about any one thing, and an infinity of equations to be worked out about an infinity of things? We are not contending that any amount of prayer can change black into white. Our contention is that the general direction which scientific research has taken in the past has varied from century to century, and that this direction has been determined by forces outside science as well as by the facts established in it. We are not saying that there is one kind of truth for the scientist and another kind for the theologian. There is but one truth. What we are asserting is that the *order* in which new knowledge about the workings of the natural creation comes into the world is important, and that this order is affected by the way the scientist prays in his work.

'Leach and Heron: Contrasting Poets'

From Eulalie's letter to Joanna 3rd July 1966

WE HAD A LONG TEA DRINKING in Bernard Leach's beautiful Japanese decorated room, looking right out on the Porthmeor Beach – and one evening he and Janet came for supper. I shall remember the hour and more on the lawn – before Janet came – when Daddy and Bernard read each other's poems – and we talked about them. The two men as different as their poetry – Bernard with his pale parchment-like skin and water-grey narrow eyes, something of the quietness of the east about him – Daddy standing up gesticulating, giving off energy like heat rays – red-brown in colour. Bernard's poetry clear, descriptive, selective, simple – like a Chinese brush drawing – Daddy's subtle, philosophical – meaning piled on meaning, needing to be brooded over, even explained.

A Revolutionary Memoir

Sparked off by the events of 1968

WHEN IN THE MIDDLE OF THE FIRST WORLD WAR the Russian Revolution broke upon us, there was a ferment which, as I recollect it, resembled in many ways the present upsurgence of students and workers – all over the world. The National Guild League, very largely the creation of a few Oxford undergraduates, had been drawing up plans for the replacement of Capitalism by an Industrial Democracy and a great many Trades Union Branches throughout the country had welcomed its speakers, who poured scorn on the talking shop known as the House of Commons and the bureaucrats who ran the industries which were then municipalized and nationalized. Everything was to be based on workshop control. The communist and anarchist ideas of William Morris and Kropotkin, and those of the French Syndicalists, were spread with a fine recklessness by men, many of whom were awaiting arrest as conscientious objectors. It was against this background that a National Conference was organised to be held in Leeds, and at this conference, the British equivalent of the Russian Council of Soldiers and Workers was to be constituted.

As the delegates, shop stewards from the Clyde, left wing Labour MPs from London and idealists of every description began to arrive, the organizers were told that lessees of the hall had cancelled the letting on the grounds that the meeting was to be held for illegal purposes. This decision was reversed when the Bradford Labour Party, who had a hall of their own, started to make arrangements for the transfer of the conference to Bradford. After an impassioned speech by the miners' leader, Bob Smillie, and some oratory by Ramsay MacDonald, Philip Snowden and William Anderson, the Workers and Soldiers Commune of Great Britain was set up and it was left to the delegates to go home and set up councils in their own districts. The only objection had come from Ernest Bevin, who, speaking from the body of the hall, had challenged the platform's sincerity. In due course I found myself in the train for Scunthorpe with three other delegates who had somehow or other got ourselves elected to the Yorkshire District Council. My companions were a Leeds Nonconformist minister, Stewart, a Labour alderman and Harold Clay, the Secretary of the Leeds Tramways Union. We were all pacifists and not one of us had the slightest idea how to set about creating a revolution!

Arriving at the Labour Club at Scunthorpe, we found a score or more other delegates waiting for us, armed ourselves with pots of beer, and elected a chairman. He was a steelmaker of enormous bulk and knew how to take his liquor. We also elected a secretary and agreed upon some sort of agenda. We had lots of 'on a point of order Mr Chairman's and the only memory I still retain of the proceedings was the chairman's reaction to a hysterical outburst from a foreign Jewish delegate from Sheffield who had said that 'this time when we get the capitalist down, there must be no talk of mercy. We must kick him in the teeth and jump on his belly and finish him off.' The Chairman, who was drinking a pint, spluttered the beer all out and shaking with laughter, kept saying 'Nay, nay, bugger it all. Nay, nay, bugger it all.'

As we never heard from London Headquarters, I called on Ramsay MacDonald at the House of Commons and was politely told to let the thing die a natural death.

Married Life at Eighty

From a letter to Joanna Nov. 19th 1970

NOW I AM GOING TO TELL YOU A STORY which I am sure will interest Rosalind. It's a true one.

Dr Lemon, that nice lady biologist in our Science Group, went into hospital last Thursday for an operation on the Friday. So we thought it would be a nice gesture to visit her and wish her some good luck. Her mother, who had come up to look after the children and who can't drive a car, asked if we would mind taking her, and of course we said we would be delighted. So we called for her ten minutes after we said we would and found her obligingly waiting on the doorstep.

Arriving at the hospital, I dropped the ladies and set off to park the car, which took me rather longer than I had thought it would. So when I got into the ward, quite a lot of the visiting time had gone. However I asked Dr Lemon if she would like me to leave an article which I knew she would want to see if she had not already read it, and as she had not, I was just on the point of taking it out of my pocket when Granny said in a very alarmed voice: 'Oh, I've left the pressure cooker on!'

Philip Mairet was staying with us so I said, 'Don't worry, I'll telephone Philip to turn it off.' In due course I found the public telephone box but it only took sixpences and shillings and I had only a two shilling piece; and unfortunately there was no machine for giving change nor any office or person near to oblige. So I went back to the ward sister at her desk, told her it was important, and I would only be a minute and she kindly broke the rules on my behalf.

The number rang alright but no Philip answered. So I begged for a directory and rang Mildred Creak next door. Again no answer, so I rang up the Prides and found they were both out – it was their daughter, Rosalind's age, who answered. When I gave her my story, the sister seemed more than slightly amused, as did the nurse who was discussing a case with her, and they were all the more amused when I had to describe to the girl firstly what a pressure cooker was, and secondly, that it was no use her knocking at the door, because the old man in the house was evidently as deaf as a stump – so she'd got to walk in boldly.

Having got her promise that she would not fail to discharge my errand, I went back to Dr Lemon, by which time I realised that the departure bell would soon be ringing. However the visit seemed to have cheered Dr Lemon up and she even seemed to be delighted when, after looking for my spectacles, I said I must have left them on the sister's desk and dashed off to recover them. Which I did.

On arriving home, we found Philip wondering whether the little girl had got the message correctly, for the pressure cooker had *not* had a light under it. I, of course, brushed this detail aside and asked why the blazes he had not answered the phone. His bland reply was that he had been listening to and viewing a space ship adventure story, and there had been lots of signals and bells ringing, and he thought it was the usual production fault of spoiling a good piece with too much incidental music and noise! I don't know what subconscious guilt it was that made your mother think she had left the light on, nor do I know what Phyllis Lemon would have thought of the article if I had left it with her. On both points an imaginative novelist would build a good story. Well, much love to you all.

The Virtue 'Hope'

All that remains of a letter to Giles on 28th May 1971

DEAR GILES,

Leila read out to me what you said to her about the virtue of Hope. It was, of course, a comfort to her to know that someone else shared her doubts about its validity as one of the three cardinal virtues. I myself have never had any misgivings. Both Faith – the belief in certainties which are unseen and immeasurable – and Hope – the expectation that in spite of all difficulties, one's desire to see these certainties given tangible form can be fulfilled – are virtues requiring the exercise of one's will; whereas Charity, when it is willed and consciously exerted, is not Charity at all; for Charity is a grace that flows naturally and is added to your environment. Neither Faith nor Hope will be required in Heaven, for then one will be face to face and there is nothing more to hope for! Incidentally, Hope will not be needed in Hell for it would not be Hell if Hope were alive in it! Of course, Hope may be hope for the wrong thing. But if it is, the results will disappoint you, and then the practical soul will try another object to hope for.

I expect you know all this. But I write because quite a short time before Joby died, I had a talk with him about de Caussade's 'Sacrament of the present moment', which some talks with my science group had illuminated for me. Mostly one goes about one's daily tasks in a kind of mechanical way – the decisions make themselves – and most of one's thoughts and movements are ordered by habit. But from time to time one encounters something NEW and then one has to make a creative decision if one is to deal with it properly. The high probability – almost certainty – which justifies habitual decisions is of no use because the NEW has not been done before. It is at these moments that, de Caussade says, one has to offer the situation up. There is no certainty that one will make the right decision, but here again one must not be presumptuous, but rather be on the look out to correct one's faults and take the opposite crossroad. Even good habits, which have stood one in good stead on other occasions, may get in one's way when one is at crossroads where the signposts have not yet been deciphered.

It is at such moments that Kirkegaard says 'Do nothing. Wait.' But whilst waiting one has to adore and praise God for everything. Unless one does this, one sinks into a depression. As one praises, one hopes. The certainty one cannot see or describe will attract one in the right direction if one but adores it and tries to do nothing else until one *has* to act. Only on such occasions is the will really free.

One must hope for these moments of enlightenment, and of course that the attainment of the practical aims which they give rise to will be for one's real advancement.

What Davidson said that set me off, was that something like this described his own attitude to research. When he came to a dead end he just stopped, put the original quest out of his head and thought about the beauty of the 'quest' itself.

Memories of Tom Heron

Extracts from the transcript of a taped interview of Ellen Bell by her social worker John Keenan recorded after Heron's death in 1983

ELLEN CAME TO THE HERONS IN 1929 PRETENDING TO BE NINETEEN. By the time they discovered she was only sixteen, they knew too much to send her home. Ellen spent the rest of her life in Welwyn Garden City.

E.B. I went to an agency in Newcastle because as you know there was no work up there and I just wanted a job so I applied to an agency and I got a job as a maid with the Herons and he met me on Valley Road because we met the coach in Newcastle and it took us right to the bottom of Valley Road and he was there with his car called the Moonbeam in them days. When I first got out of the coach I was a little in awe of Mr Heron because he had got a beard and I thought he was a Jew and we were brought up to dislike Jews ... no reason of my own but that's how we were brought up and I said I don't want to go to your house I want to go back you're a Jew and he promptly said 'Ellen I am not a Jew but there is nothing wrong with the Jews. Come just give us a try out.' So off he went in his car and we went to 31 Valley Road, and that was the first house I worked for him.

Sometimes Mrs Heron went out to music classes and left me to it or she would go in the evening to bible classes and leave me to look after the children and I used to sit on the bed, tell them stories or eat apples or various things and we had a real good time with the children and all of a sudden I thought 'what a lovely life. I am glad I came here.'

Whenever she had to go out it was all right I took care of things, collected the children from school and on the whole I was terribly happy there, so, and I never wanted to leave. I'd never known a life like I had with Mr and Mrs Heron. I was very unhappy at home but well they were like my parents John, that's how I felt about them and every time they had a holiday they took me with them.

We were not allowed boy friends, not in the north, not at my age, Oh no.

J.K. But the Herons allowed you to have boy friends.

E.B. Yes they did. I told Mr and Mrs Heron I'd got a boy friend and they said well if you've got a boy friend Ellen don't keep him hidden away. We'd like you to bring him to the house because you are very young you know and we don't want anything to happen to you. So right I brought AG to the house to see the Herons. And when I told them we had nowhere to go because the disco wasn't on – bring him here make him a cup of tea, and you can have the kitchen.

J.K. And after having several boy friends you finally met ...

E.B. Yes I finally met one who I married. And he was allowed to go to their home all the time. We got married from their house and his name was Harold and Mrs Heron and Mr Heron came to the Registry Office and stood in, you know and she gave me a big bunch of red carnations.

J.K. Who gave you away?

E.B. They gave me away. Then the war came and I was having the children. I only had three to my first husband and then he got killed I told you and Mr and Mrs Heron were the godparents and they helped me all they could. They said 'Bring the children and come up to my house, bring the children with you.' They'd got a swing, a dell, everything there and the children played up there and she kept going out and telling them stories. She was a wonderful woman. She could make up wonderful stories.

J.K. So, looking back, did you think of them more like parents?

E.B. I do, more like foster parents. I liked them better than my parents. It's hard to say it. I loved my Mum in my way because I was sorry for her but I was never sorry I left them.

J.K. Your home was with the Herons.

E.B. The police came to take me away because I was under age and the Herons stepped in and helped me again ... Whatever he said and whatever he did I don't know but whatever he did I was allowed to stay with the Herons.
  He was the finest man I ever knew and I loved him a great deal. Mrs Heron always knows. I loved Mrs Heron but Mr Heron ... there was something special between us. He saved me. I always remember saving me from going back to that place. I never had to go back home any more.

J.K. There were sad times, bad times?

E.B. After I got married he came up to London to collect me from the hospital when I was ill and he brought me back. They never bought luxuries, They made do with what they'd got – they had the same things all the time, didn't have new things. They went to church. I went to take the bread and the wine with them sometimes, to St Francis'. The Vicar came to tell me Mr Heron was dead. They thought it best. Lloyd Jones. He brought me a letter at 8.30. one night. I couldn't believe it. They had a service at St Francis'. My daughter came with me. He was a father to me. In Mr Heron's last letter he said, 'always thank God if anything happens to me that He's let me have you for so long.' He must have known he was dying. 'Ellen don't grieve too much. I've had a wonderful life with Mrs Heron.'

Judas

There had to be a Judas
choosing and chosen
to complete the Twelve,
choosing and chosen
to betray the Christ.
There had to be a Judas
to fulfil the Word.

Now am I glorified.

I try to pray for Judas
cast for his tragic part,
but there's no image to inform my prayer.
Would not the Christ himself have had compassion
had aught remained
of man or matter
after that headlong fall?

They say that Judas prized his messianic dream
more than he prized the Love Incarnate;
and I too know this wilfulness,
yet know I can be shriven!

Judas, they say, bemused as Abraham was,
heard God's voice and obeyed,
daring to test his own and Christ's integrity,
but saw no ram.

Yet doubting Thomas was forgiven,
and Peter of three denials
is canonized. Is there not logic in
the African's Saint Judas?

No explanation can contain this story.
It is a living thing
and changes with our growth
and for our need.
The bowels gushing forth beneath the Judas tree
are tortured atoms now
under a mushroom cloud.
Yet always the still centre of the tale proclaims –
Now am I glorified!

20th July 1962

Golden Wedding

Birdsong and children's laughter
and contrapuntally
the boom of guns from Passchendaele
these were the sounds we heard when strangely drawn
we came upon The Woods of Westermain
just fifty years ago.
Oh they were golden then
as they are golden now
and we two dared to come to terms with magic.

The snake across our path
stretched in his golden bath
and we begrudged him not the sun.

So was it once in Eden,
just Nature holding sway.
But Westermain was planted when The Fall
entangled good and evil in new birth.
And there beside us the old serpent lay.

We stirred.
The yaffle's mocking cry
assailed the lark on high
yet did not dim its ecstasy.

That was enough. By this we knew
our path lay through the woods.
Oh they were golden then
as they are golden now
and shall be every fall
before the dark of winter purchases
another Spring.
Then will the lark high soar as if to bring
new gold from Saturn for another wedding ring,
and though the warning bird croak harsh 'Hiroshima'
the lark will sing.

17th September 1968

Tom and Eulalie celebrating their Golden Wedding: September 1968.

Zennor Head

The guilty conscience of a restless age
that knows exactly where typhoons will strike
and spell-bound waits for their approach
does not depress the hares that play on Zennor Head,
nor does the anguish that we call America
deter the setting sun from lavishing
its bounty on the sea that takes it there.

But Zennor Head is not all innocence.
Those ancient rocks, massive placidity,
once boiled in protest at intolerable pain,
then burst right through the Earth's protective crust
to pour their wrath into a boiling sea –
the over-spill still works in hawk and adder
and in the shudder we call Equinox.

I turn towards the East. Another granite pile
shares the contentment of this halcyon sea.
Rocks that earth travailed to bring forth
were rent and hewn to build a village church,
enriching consciousness that was of water born.
I think of Patmos and the vision clear
of jewels that the past is gathering here.

May–June 1970

Opposite: Drawing by Patrick Heron in T.M. Heron's *Call it a Day*.

Sections from Brack Ross Holiday
An Allegorical Diary

I

Movements of Life in Death
and Death in Life.
Just sky and sea and rocks
lovemaking with each other.
Beauty in Silence sings
Silence in Beauty glows.
I join the birds and trees and rocks
and find myself
in Church.

That hillside, gully cleft,
lies open like the Book
placed on the lectern for today's First Lesson,
to read it my appointed task.
It is the story of events,
Small Man protecting Nature from herself
by building barns and walls and digging ditches.
Those animals now live at peace with one another
and with the rest of God's Creation.
That sheepdog now contains the wolf.

How strange the scheme of things.
That gnarled old twisted tree
rooted on prehistoric rock
enjoys God's peace,
its stubborn foliage my text,
Holy Fertility.
That wayside statue hewn in rugged rock –
Mary the Virgin all alone
holds in her womb my argument
waiting in labour to be born.

II

Another day.
Soft clouds on distant hills.
Mist curling aimlessly as it descends
with water for the miracle of wine

and for all natural transformation.
How comely Nature is!
No sooner said —
I race for shelter from the pelting rain
and think again.

I know another cloud, another world.
Beyond those hills the population spawns,
production runs amok,
the priests of Baal flaunt their G.N.P.
as money copulates and breeds like vermin.
Litter accumulates,
vaunting abundance chokes variety
and chaos ceases to dismay.
Only a second Deluge
can wash this filth away.

But no.
I saw a rainbow yesterday.
Besides
did not the Virgin's holy rock
once boil in molten discontent
beneath an angry sea?
Love now can trust a gentler way.
In Anno Domini
Man came of age.

May–June–July 1974

Nature and Supernature

A tree allots its sap
to stem and leaf and flower and seed,
and to its roots adventuring in the dark
assigns the strength they need to play their part.

At peace within its sovereign realm,
content to be the tree
God gave it life to be,
an oak may stand three hundred years
producing timber for man's art
and by example teaching him that he
must look for Beauty in Economy.

Good oaks live on in heaven's eternal groves,
and oaken consciousness looks down
on lovely minsters with their oaken beams
and oaken rood-lofts holding up the tree
that bears the Christ in Glory.
How all-embracing is Creation's plan
and how magnificent the rôle assigned to Man!

1975

By Way of Introduction

My world extends beyond the bounds of time and space.
Its centre is the soul
a ring without circumference.
Its language is the pregnant word
in poem and prophecy.
Its light is darkness vanishing
and leaving all things new,
its beauty spontaneity,
its time part of eternity,
its sound the music of the spheres
only in silence heard.

All this my private property
the planet that I hold in fee
shares in the glory of the galaxies
that circulate Creation.

Reader in Mars or nearest neighbour
am I opaque to you as you to me?
My simple art sends salutations.
Some day we shall be one.

26th July 1976

Cause and Chance

Thank God for the uncertainty of life.
Plans are frustrated,
machinery breaks down.
So God creates the space for his manœuvre.
We call it chance.

And thank God for the certainty of death,
for obsolescence and redundancy,
for new discovery and research.
So God creates the space for man's manœuvre
in quest of cause.

What causes chance, or what strange hap
set primal cause in motion, who can tell?
Only in God-like spontaneity
do cause and chance meet and make sense.
Thank God for everything.

1977

Tom Heron – Bibliography

Books

Call it a Day. Poems Ark Press 1977

Pamphlets

Christian Vocation in Industry and Marketing Cath. Lit. Assoc. 1926
    Anglo-Catholic Congress Books No. 16 General Introduction by Bishop Charles Gore
The Relation of Freedom and Control in Industry I. C. F. 1943
    Address to Council of the Industrial Christian Fellowship, Westminster on 23 September 1943
Prolegomena to the Methodology of the Study of Unnecessary Sweat N.E.W. 1945
    First published in *The New English Weekly* 22 February, 1945
What has Christianity to say on Leisure in the Modern State? I.C.F. 1949
    Address in Southwark Cathedral on 20 May 1949 in connection with the Mission to London.
Will Automation Cause Unemployment? I.C.F. 1957
Christian Living in an Expanding Economy Church Union 1957
    Syllabus for Thirty-Second Summer School of Sociology

Books – Contribution to composite work

Man at Work in *Prospect for Christendom* Faber & Faber 1945
    Essays in Catholic Social Reconstruction Edited by Maurice B. Reckitt

Essays, Articles and Letters (of interest or importance) in Journals and Periodicals.

G.K's Weekly

Letter *The Area of the Market* July 16 1927

Christendom (A Journal of Christian Sociology)

Article *Work, Leisure and the Creation* March 1936
Article *The Function of Industry in a Town* March 1942
    A paper read at the Oxford Summer School of Sociology
Article *The Function of Industry and the Machine* June 1942
    Expanded from an address to the Summer School of Sociology
Article *The Welfare State* March 1947
    Closing address to Church Union Summer School of Sociology, Oxford in 1946 Part I
    Article as above Part 2 September 1947

The New English Weekly (Heron's contributions were sometimes under pseudonyms – 'Ealdorman', 'Aeldoman' and 'H')

Article *Leisure* April 29 1937
Article *Pure Fiction* November 2 1939

Letter *Education for Leadership?* November 2 1939
Letter *Abolish Unemployment* December 19 1940
Letter *Wages and 'Vicious Spiral'* January 2 1941
Letter *Social Credit during War* July 17 1941
Letter *Religion, Politics and Government* Sept. 10 1942
Article *A Peep at P.E.P.* September 16 1943
Article *Cartels and Conscience* November 18 1943
Letter *Cartels* December 2 1943
Article *'Inflation on the Widest Scale'* April 13 1944
Article/Review *Lend-Lease Empire Building* June 22 1944
   (*Including review of Lend-Lease Weapon for Victory* by E. R. Stettinus)
Article/Review *The Pax Americana* November 16 1944
   (Including review of *The Time for Decision* by Sumner Welles)
Article *Prolegomena to the Methodology of the Study of Unnecessary Sweat* February 22 1945
   (also published as pamphlet)
Letter *Post-War Trade* September 20 1945
Letter *Words, Things and Money* December 28 1945
Letter *A National Wages Policy* June 27 1946
Letter *Lease and Lend* April 3 1941
Review *Management and Men* by G. S. Walpole March 8 1945

Wealth (A review of news and opinions of service for all students of the reaction of economic principles to human welfare)

Article *Money's True Function* November 1937
   (Address given at Christ Church, Victoria Street, London October 21 1937)

Christian News-Letter (Christian Frontier Council)

Article/Supplement *The Incentive to Work* January 1947
Article *Moral Re-Armament* April 1955
   (on the Report of the Social and Industrial Council of the Church Assembly)

Frontier (Incorporating Christian News-Letter and World Dominion)

Article *The Human Factor in Large Scale Industry* November 1951
Review *Sex in Christianity and Psychoanalysis* by William Graham Cole January 1958
Letter *Unemployment* January 1959
Article *God and the Spontaneous* Winter 1960
Poem *To Bertrand Russell* (2 February 1970) June 1970

Prism (Anglican Monthly)

Letter *The Church and Art* April 1959
Letter *The Church and Art* June 1959

Anglican Theological Review (U. S. A.)

Article *Towards the Redemption of Science* January 1961

The Guardian (A Weekly Church newspaper)

Article *Vocation, Life and Work* April 10 1941
   (Paper read at Malvern Conference 1941)

The Pottery Gazette and Glass Trade Review

Article *Some Thoughts on Post-War Reconstruction* September 1943
   (Also printed separately)

Theology

Review *Pour une theologie du travail* by M. D. Chenu May 1956
Article *The Sane Society and the Kingdom of God* November 1956
Review *Christianity and Economic Problems* by D. L. Munby August 1957

Theoria to Theory

Poem *Peacock Science* January 1967
Review/Discussion *The Parable of the Beast* by John Bleibtreu December 1968

Miscellaneous

Monetary Policy. A Manifesto from a Christian Standpoint Published by Christian Social Council
   1936. Tom Heron chaired the committee which produced it.
Monetary Steps towards a Better Social Order. Statement adopted at the close of a week-end
   Conference of Christian economists and businessmen meeting at Haywards Heath in June 1937.
   Tom Heron chaired the Conference.

Major or Feature Articles

A great many of Heron's articles appeared over the years in newspapers and periodicals, including
   The Spectator, New Statesman, The Humanist, The Church Times, The Liberator, The Month, The
   (Bradford) *Telegraph and Argus, The Kent Messenger, The Sheffield Morning Telegraph, CR*
   Quarterly ... and much, much more.

Index

With no disrespect for subsequent honours, this index adopts the personal styles used in the text, those familar to Heron himself.